Workplace
Spanish

Second Edition

Leslie A. Holloway
Grace S. Thomson

Workplace *ESL* Solutions

ISBN 13: 978-0-9743660-0-5
ISBN 10: 0-9743660-0-5

Printed in the United States of America

Second Printing: October 2006

10 09 08 07 06   6 5 4 3 2

For information or to order additional books or CDs,
visit: www.WorkplaceESL.com
or call (702) 873-3520.

Workplace ESL Solutions Publishing Company
55 South Valle Verde 235-110
Henderson, NV 89012

Dear Teacher:

Welcome to the second edition of Workplace Spanish. We have made significant changes to each Lección, including new activities that will help your students with their pronunciation, grammar and writing skills. We have added more ESTRUCTURE notes and have redone our audio CD set and teacher's guide.

In this textbook, employees will learn to communicate with other employees, clients and customers in Spanish through authentic workplace conversations. Vocabulary and situations are presented in a clear and concise manner to facilitate easy understanding and use by the first time learner.

Workplace Spanish presents 10 lessons focusing on basic Spanish vocabulary and some grammar. It is intended to encourage learners to express ideas in Spanish about specific workplace topics and real life situations. You will find a variety of exercises and activities throughout the text to enhance the communicative use of the language.

This book has an audio CD set to practice speaking/listening and pronunciation.

To send us your suggestions or for additional information about *Workplace Spanish*, *Workplace English*, or *Hotel English* products, please visit our website at *www.WorkplaceESL.com*.

Thank you.

Leslie A. Holloway
Grace S. Thomson

Acknowledgements

Grace Thomson is the master behind this second edition. Ronna Timpa, CEO and founder of Workplace ESL Solutions, hired Grace in 2004 to teach Workplace Spanish, and she quickly became one of the best instructors her company had ever seen. Denise Aguilar helped to edit the book.

The following people helped with the editing and/or production of our first edition: Aaron Nitzkin, Ronna Timpa, Lyn Pizor, Connie Izquierdo, Paul Franzmann and Magaly Toledo.

Whether you have practiced Spanish for a long time or you are starting right now, there are some tips that you need to know about the Spanish language. These tips will help you with the pronunciation and the basic skills to read Spanish.

Let´s start with what we call the "easy five". The sounds of the vowels in Spanish. You will be amazed at learning that you just need to know five primary sounds and you will be reading Spanish as an expert! Here they are:

a (ah)   like map

e (eh)   like met

i (ee)   like keep

o (oh)   like open

u (oo)   like spoon

The sounds in Spanish are made with the front of your mouth instead of the back. The sounds are crisp, brief and choppy. Practice as much as you can. Try reading these words:

agua   auto   casa   mamá   comida   dinero

Now let´s practice the ALFABETO in Spanish.

   Escuche y repita.

A	*ah*	**J**	*hoh-tah*	**R**	*eh-reh*
B	*beh*	**K**	*kah*	**S**	*eh-seh*
C	*seh*	**L**	*el-leh*	**T**	*teh*
D	*deh*	**M**	*em-meh*	**U**	*oo*
E	*eh*	**N**	*en-neh*	**V**	*veh*
F	*eh-feh*	**Ñ**	*en-nyeh*	**W**	*doblay-veh*
G	*heh*	**O**	*oh*	**X**	*eh-kees*
H	*ah-cheh*	**P**	*peh*	**Y**	*yeh*
I	*ee*	**Q**	*koo*	**Z**	*seh-tah*

Alfabeto (alphabet)

The Spanish alphabet has 27 letters:

26 letters of the English alphabet + ñ

Previously the Spanish alphabet had 3 two-letter combinations (ch, ll, rr). They are now considered to be part of the letters c, l and r and will be listed that way in most dictionaries. However in older dictionaries and for spelling purposes, these letters may still be used.

COMMUNICATION GOALS:	To meet and greet other people
	To ask someone to spell their name
	To use expressions of courtesy
STRUCTURE:	Formal vs. Informal You (Ud. vs. Tú)
PRONUNCIATION:	The alphabet – Consonants/Vowels
	Accent marks
CULTURAL FOCUS:	Greetings in the Hispanic world

¿Sabía Ud?

Puerto Rico, a commonwealth of the United States, has its own constitution. Its people are citizens of the United States, follow the same federal laws, and use the dollar as their monetary unit. The island is about the same size as the two states of Rhode Island and Delaware combined. About one million Puerto Ricans live in the United States, the majority of whom reside in New York City.

The Puerto Ricans have two national anthems, two flags, and celebrate both Puerto Rican and American holidays. However, the official language is Spanish.

Conversación
Escuche.

Diálogo 1.1

> Juan: Hola, buenos días.
> David: Buenos días.
> Juan: ¿Cómo estás?
> David: Bien, gracias. ¿Y tú?
> Juan: Muy bien, gracias.
> David: Bien, hasta luego.
> Juan: Adiós.

Diálogo 1.2

> María: Hola, buenas tardes.
> Lupe: Buenas tardes.
> Me llamo Lupe Sánchez.
> ¿Cómo se llama?
> María: Me llamo María Martínez.
> Lupe: Mucho gusto.
> María: El gusto es mío.

Diálogo 1.3

> Raúl: Buenas tardes.
> Ricardo: Muy buenas tardes. Me
> llamo Ricardo Mendoza.
> ¿Cómo se llama usted?
> Raúl: Me llamo Raúl Santos. Trabajo
> en el hotel. Soy botones.
> ¿Dónde trabaja usted?
> Ricardo: Trabajo en el hotel también.
> Soy cajero.
> Raúl: Mucho gusto.
> Ricardo: Encantado. Hasta luego.
> Raúl: Adiós.

Actividad A: Escuche y repita: Escuche cada diálogo y repita.

Actividad B: En parejas, lea cada diálogo.

Actividad C: Haga una lista de expresiones para cada columna. Escoja las palabras de los diálogos de la página 2.

Saludos:	Despedidas:
1.	1.
2.	2.
3.	3.
4.	4.

Actividad D: ¿Cómo responde? Use el vocabulario de las conversaciones para responder.

Por ejemplo: *¿Cómo estás?*
Bien, gracias.

A: ¿Qué tal?   B:

A: ¿Me llamo Raúl. ¿Y tú? B:

A: ¿Dónde trabajas?   B:

A: Hola, buenos días.   B:

A: Bien, gracias. ¿Y tú?   B:

A: Adiós.   B:

A: Mucho gusto.   B:

Actividad E: Asociaciones: Asocie el vocabulario en español de la primera columna con el inglés de la segunda columna.

Columna 1

1. soy
2. Me llamo
3. botones
4. ¿Y tú?
5. ¿Cómo te llamas?
6. Mucho gusto
7. también
8. ¿Qué tal?
9. Quiero presentarle a mi amigo.
10. Trabajo
11. Bien, gracias.
12. El gusto es mío.
13. ¿Dónde trabajas?
14. Encantado(a)
15. ¿Cómo estás?
16. cajero

Columna 2

___5___ What's your name?
___8___ How are things going?
___7___ too, also
___13___ Where do you work?
___10___ I work
___6___ Pleased to meet you. (1)
___2___ My name is
___3___ bellboy
___15___ How are you?
___1___ I am
___9___ I'd like you to meet my friend.
___11___ Fine, thanks.
___14___ Pleased to meet you. (2)
___12___ The pleasure is mine.
___4___ And you?
___16___ cashier

Nota Cultural:

Greeting relatives and acquaintances is a very important custom among Hispanic people. Everyone greets each other, adults, children, friends, and neighbors. Even when it means interrupting conversations or activities, people always greet one another. Generally, greetings include physical contact. Men and boys often include hand shakes, hugging, and a pat on the back; a soft kiss on the cheek may also be exchanged among women and girls.

Expresiones útiles: Practique estás expresiones y úselas diariamente para aprenderlas bien. Escuche y repita:

And you?	¿Y usted? ¿Y tú?
Bless you!	¡Salud!
Excuse me.	Con permiso. (used when interrupting)
Fine, thanks.	Bien, gracias.
Go ahead.	Pase.
I'm sorry!	¡Lo siento!
Please	Por favor
Thanks a lot.	Muchas gracias.
What's happening?	¿Qué pasa?
You're welcome.	De nada.

Pronunciación:

1. You may have noticed accent marks in certain words of the conversation. Accent marks are part of the Spanish spelling. They should not be left out.

2. Where does the accent fall if it is not marked on the word? If the word ends in a vowel, n or s, the accent or stress falls on the second to last syllable. If the word ends in any other consonant (not n or s), the stress falls on the last syllable.

    For example: Escuche y repita: p**a**sa, c**i**nco, m**a**dre, herm**a**nos, abu**e**los españ**o**l, libert**a**d, elem**e**ntal, habl**a**r

    Any word that does not follow one of these two rules will have the accent mark written over the vowel that gets the stress. REMEMBER: Only **vowels** can have an accent mark.

3. In Spanish, question marks and exclamation points occur at the beginning and end of a question or exclamation. They are written at the place where the question or exclamation begin and indicate to the speaker to change his intonation at the end of the question or exclamation.

Tarea (Homework):

1. Practice the dialogs at the beginning of the chapter.

2. Study the meanings and pronunciation of the vocabulary and useful expressions.

3. Make time twice a week to practice with another Spanish student.

4. Make a date for lunch or break time and practice with a Spanish speaking friend.

5. When entering or leaving the classroom, use an appropriate Spanish greeting to address your teacher.

 ## Vocabulario Lección 1:
Escuche y Repita.

Hola	Hi
Buenos dias	Good morning
Buenas tardes	Good afternoon
Buenas noches	Good evening
¿Cómo estás?	How are you? (informal)
¿Qué tal?	How's it going?
Bien, gracias.	Fine thanks.
Muy bien	Very well
¿Cómo te llamas?	What's your name? (informal)
Me llamo…	My name is…
¿Y tú?	And you? (informal)
Mucho gusto	Pleased to meet you.
El gusto es mío.	The pleasure is mine.
Encantado(a).	Pleased to meet you.
¿Dónde trabajas?	Where do you work?
Trabajo en…	I work at…
soy…	I am…
botones	bellboy
cajero	cashier
también	also, too
Adiós.	Goodbye.
Hasta mañana.	See you tomorrow.
Hasta luego.	See you later.
Quiero presentarle a mi amigo(a)…	I would like to introduce my friend to you.
saludos	greetings
despedidas	farewells

COMMUNICATION GOALS:	To tell time
	To ask and answer number questions
	To ask how much
STRUCTURE:	¿Qué hora es?
	¿Cuánto cuesta(n)?
PRONUNCIATION:	Las vocales
CULTURAL FOCUS:	Time and Money

¿Sabía Ud?

In 1994, **Cubans** were permitted to experiment in self-enterprise. They were allowed to convert part of their homes into a small restaurant (no more than 12 seats) serving Cuban home-cooking. Since then, many became commercialized and expensive. Look for *paladars* in residential areas rather than tourist areas to avoid over charging. Meals should cost no more than $5 to $10 per person.

Conversación:
Escuche.

Diálogo 2.1

Raúl y Pablo están en la oficina. Ellos hablan.

Raúl:	Hola, Me llamo Raúl. ¿Cómo se llama?
Pablo:	Me llamo Pablo.
Raúl:	Mucho gusto. Tengo su solicitud aquí pero todavía necesito su número de teléfono. ¿Cuál es?
Pablo:	Mi número de teléfono es 897-4360.

Diálogo 2.2

El camarero escucha a las clientes. Ellos están en un restaurante.

Cliente:	¿Cuánto cuesta una coca-cola?
Camarero:	¿Una coca-cola? Cuesta 95 centavos.
Cliente:	¿Y una hamburguesa?
Camarero:	Una hamburguesa cuesta $2.00 dólares. Entonces una soda con una hamburguesa cuestan $2.95.
Cliente:	Gracias.
Camarero:	De nada.

Diálogo 2.3

Dos personas esperan en una cola antes del concierto del grupo, "Los Tigres."

María:	¿Qué hora es?
Pilar:	Son las dos y diez (2:10).
María:	¿Y a qué hora empieza el concierto?
Pilar:	El concierto empieza a las siete (7:00) de la noche y termina a las diez y media (10:30) de la noche.
María:	Gracias.
Pilar:	No hay de qué.

Actividad A: Escuche y repita: Escuche cada diálogo.

Actividad B: En parejas, lea cada diálogo.

Actividad C: Identifique el vocabulario. Asociaciones. Dibuje una línea entre la palabra y el dibujo correcto.

El concierto

La hamburguesa

El refresco

Son las 10:30.

El teléfono

Los centavos

(847) 415-4105

Los dólares

El número de teléfono

¿Cuánto cuesta?

Los Números:

Escuche y Repita:

0	cero
1	uno
2	dos
3	tres
4	cuatro
5	cinco
6	seis
7	siete
8	ocho
9	nueve
10	diez
11	once
12	doce
13	trece
14	catorce
15	quince
16	diez y seis (dieciséis)
17	diez y siete (diecisiete)
18	diez y ocho (dieciocho)
19	diez y nueve (diecinueve)
20 (21)	veinte (veinte y uno – veintiuno)
30 (32)	treinta (treinta y dos)
40 (43)	cuarenta (cuarenta y tres)
50 (54)	cincuenta (cincuenta y cuatro)
60 (65)	sesenta (sesenta y cinco)
70 (76)	setenta (setenta y seis)
80 (87)	ochenta (ochenta y siete)
90 (98)	noventa (noventa y ocho)
100 (109)	cien, ciento (ciento nueve)
1,000	mil
2,000	dos mil
10,000	diez mil
100,000	cien mil
1,000,000	un millón

Estructura: La Hora

To ask what time it is in Spanish we say: ¿Qué hora es?

To tell time in Spanish, we use *Es* before the number 1 and *Son* for all other times.

> **Es** la una. It is one o'clock.
> **Son** las dos. It is two o'clock.

To tell the numbers of minutes past the hour, say the hour plus *y* the number of minutes.

> **Es** la una **y** diez. It is 1:10.
> **Son** las tres **y** veinticinco. It is 3:25.

Quarter after the hour can be stated by using the number fifteen (quince) or the word quarter (cuarto).

> Es la una y **quince**. Es la una y **cuarto**. It is 1:15.
> Son las seis y **quince**. Son las seis y **cuarto**. It is 6:15.

Thirty minutes past the hour can be expressed by the words *y treinta* or *y media*.

> Es la una y **treinta**. Es la una y **media**. It is 1:30.
> Son las ocho y **treinta**. Son las ocho y **media**. It is 8:30.

¿A qué hora?

Telling at what time something begins or ends is expressed by adding the word *A* at the beginning of a phrase.

> ¿A qué hora es la fiesta? La fiesta es **a** las dos.
> At what time is the party? The party is at 2:00.

To express AM and PM:

> De la mañana—until noon
> De la tarde—noon until 7:00 pm
> De la noche—7:00 pm until midnight

Actividad D: ¿Qué hora es? Dígalo en español.

1. 2:35 a.m.
2. 3:15 p.m.
3. 5:00 p.m.
4. 9:00 a.m.
5. 4:45 p.m.
6. 6:05 a.m.
7. 8:12 p.m.
8. 7:10 a.m.
9. 1:50 p.m.
10. 11:27 p.m.

Actividad E: En parejas, pregunte y responda según la hora en el reloj.

Por Ejemplo:
Estudiante 1: ¿A qué hora es la clase de español?
Estudiante 2: A las ocho y cuarenta y cinco (8:45).

1.  ¿el almuerzo?

_____

2.  ¿el vuelo?

_____

3.  ¿la cita?

_____

4.  ¿la salida?

_____

5.  ¿la reunión?

_____

6.  ¿la fiesta?

_____

Actividad F. Pregunte y conteste:

1. ¿Cuál es su número de teléfono? Ex. <u>Mi número de teléfono es 702-232-2954</u>

2. ¿Cuál es su número de habitación? _____

3. ¿Cuál es su número de identificación? _____

4. ¿Cuál es su número de cuenta? _____

5. ¿Cuál es su número de mesa? _____

Estructura: ¿Cuánto Cuesta?

To ask about prices in Spanish, we say: *¿Cuánto Cuesta?*

To say the prices, we say the amount in dollars followed by the word *y* and the amount in cents.

Cuesta ocho dólares y cincuenta centavos ($8.50).

Actividad G: Pregunte y conteste:

Let's practice saying prices in Spanish.

¿Cuánto cuesta la soda? ($2.40)

La soda cuesta 2 (dos) dólares y 40 (cuarenta) centavos.

¿Cuánto cuesta ....?

  la lámpara $15.00

 el carro $25,000

  el libro $24.60

  la solicitud $1.99

  el pastel $5.80

  La cerveza $2.50

  El permiso $22.00

Actividad H: Cuente de 2 en 2: 2, 4, 6, etc.
Cuente de 5 en 5: 5, 10, etc.
Cuente de 10 en 10: 10, 20, etc.

Actividad I: Crucigrama

Across

1. one
3. twelve
6. zero
8. thirteen
13. thirty
15. nine
16. ninety
18. five
19. three
20. six
21. fifty
22. ten

Down

2. eleven
4. fourteen
5. twenty
7. eighty
9. fifteen
10. forty
11. seventy
12. sixty
14. seven
17. two
18. four
21. one hundred

¿Nota Cultural: A qué hora comemos?

The meal schedule in Latino countries is very different from what is familiar to Americans. Although breakfast is eaten at times generally similar to the United States, between 6:00 and 9:00 in the morning, Hispanic people eat lunch, often the day's largest meal, between 1:00 and 2:00 in the afternoon. Much like "tea time" in the United Kingdom, Latinos frequently enjoy a light snack between 5:00 p.m. and 6:00 p.m. consisting of coffee or tea and a pastry or small sandwich. Dinner is usually eaten considerably later in Hispanic countries than in the United States. It is not unusual to sit down to dinner between 8:00 and 9:00 in the evening. In Spain, dinner may be even later, between 10:00 p.m. and midnight. At that time, a small meal is served, often leftovers from lunch.

¿Cuánto cuesta?

Although Hispanic people share the same language, currencies vary from country to country. Many countries name their currency the *peso*, although the value of each *peso* may vary. Mexico, Argentina, and Bolivia all call their money *el peso*. Ecuador's monetary unit is *el dólar* since 2000. This is one of the two Latin American countries that have the dollar as their currency. The other one is Costa Rica. You shop with *el quetzal* in Guatemala; in Venezuela, you spend *el Bolívar*.

Expresiones Útiles: Practique estas expresiones y úselas diariamente para aprenderlas bien. Escuche y repita:

Congratulations!	¡Felicitaciones!
Be careful!	¡Tenga cuidado!
Do you need help?	¿Necesita ayuda?
Good job!	¡Buen trabajo!
Have a nice day.	Qué le vaya bien.
I don't understand.	No comprendo.
What a shame!	¡Qué lástima!

Pronunciación: Las Vocales A and E

1. The letter **"a"** in Spanish is always pronounced like the **a** in **"ha-ha."** Unlike English vowel sounds, Spanish vowels have only one sound. The vowel sounds are short, clipped and never drawn out.

   Escuche y repita: banana mapa lata casa sala

2. The sound of the letter **e** in Spanish is like the **"eh"** sound in the English word **pen.**

   Escuche y repita: mete deme teme pese bebé

Tarea (Homework):

1. Practice the dialogs at the beginning of the chapter.

2. Study the meanings and pronunciation of the new vocabulary and useful expressions.

3. Count by 2's, 3's, 5's, and 10's.

4. Practice saying your house number, social security number and zip code in Spanish.

Vocabulario Lección 2:
Escuche y Repita.

¿Cuál es su número de teléfono?	What is your phone number?
mi/su	my/your
es	is
¿Cuánto cuesta?	How much does something cost?
cuesta(n)	It costs (they cost)
una coca-cola	a coke
una hamburguesa	a hamburger
dólares	dollars
centavos	cents
pesos	monetary unit used in several Latin American countries
así	so
¿Qué hora es?	What time is it?
Es la una.	It is one o'clock.
Son las dos, tres etc.	It is two o'clock, three o'clock etc.
y	and
menos	minus
cuarto	quarter
media	half
empieza	it starts
termina	it ends
¿A qué hora?	At what time?
a las	at
el concierto	the concert
de la mañana	A.M. (morning until noon)
de la tarde	P.M. (afternoon until 6:59 p.m.)
de la noche	P.M. (evening after 7:00 p.m.)
No hay de qué.	It's nothing.

COMMUNICATION GOALS:	To give orders and advice
	To use expressions of courtesy
STRUCTURE:	Affirmative commands or imperative mode
PRONUNCIATION:	Las vocales
CULTURAL FOCUS:	Los Hispanos in the United States

¿Sabía Ud?

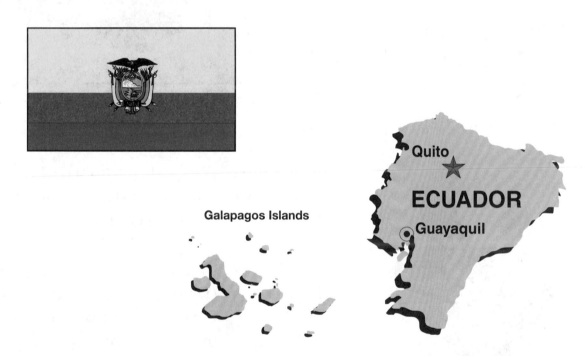

Quito

ECUADOR

Guayaquil

Galapagos Islands

True Panama hats are indeed made in **Ecuador**, but how did such a misnomer come about?

In the mid-1800's, gold-seekers rushing to California by way of the Isthmus of Panama purchased hats imported from Ecuador. In time, the hats came to be known by the name of their point of purchase rather than their place of origin.

A genuine Panama hat is light, airy, and lasts a lifetime. Each is hand-woven and therefore one of a kind. Prices range from a few dollars for coarser hats to more than $1,000 for the rarest, softest weave.

It's good to remember, a *genuine* Panama hat is made only in Ecuador, and it's called "sombrero de Montecristi."

Conversación
Escuche.

Diálogo 3.1

Un hombre quiere comer pero no sabe dónde está el restaurante.

Un hombre:	Perdone. ¿Dónde está el restaurante El Toro?
Otro hombre:	Está cerca de aquí. Vaya derecho hasta la esquina. En la esquina, doble a la izquierda. Está allí al lado del correo.
Un hombre:	Muchas gracias.
Otro hombre:	De nada.

Diálogo 3.2

Una mujer necesita hablar con el gerente.

La secretaria:	¿En qué le puedo servir?
Una mujer:	Por favor, ¿Está el gerente?
La secretaria:	El señor Martín está ocupado. Espere un momento y siéntese.
Una mujer:	Gracias.
La secretaria:	(Después de unos minutos) El Sr. Martín puede hablar con usted ahora. Venga conmigo. Gracias por su paciencia.
Una mujer:	De nada.

Diálogo 3.3

Ya son las nueve de la mañana y la familia Rojas está atrasada.

Mamá:	¡Apúrate mi hija!
La hija:	Mamá. No puedo.
Mamá:	Escucha mi hija, es tarde.
La hija:	Bueno mamá, ya voy.

Actividad A: Escuche y repita: Escuche y repita cada diálogo.

Actividad B: En parejas, lea cada diálogo.

Actividad C: Estudie los tres diálogos. ¿Puede encontrar las órdenes y las palabras de cortesía en cada diálogo? Haga una lista y luego compare su lista con la de su compañero.

Palabras de cortesía:	Órdenes o imperativos:
1.	1.
2.	2.
3.	3.
4.	4.
5.	5.

Actividad D: Conteste las siguientes preguntas.

Diálogo 1:
1. ¿Cómo se llama el restaurante?
2. ¿Está el restaurante cerca o lejos?
3. ¿Qué está al lado del restaurante?

Diálogo 2:
1. ¿Dónde están estas personas?
2. ¿Quién es el gerente?
3. ¿Por qué espera la mujer??

Diálogo 3:
1. ¿Quiénes hablan en esta conversación?
2. ¿Por qué tiene prisa la mamá?

Actividad E: Usando las frases para dar instrucciones, diga:
¿Cómo responde Ud. en estas situaciones? En español, ¡claro!

1. You work in a hotel and a guest is obviously lost.
2. You need to interrupt a conversation.
3. You accidentally bump into someone.
4. A customer has been waiting a long time to speak to you.
5. Someone thanks you for your help.

Estructura: Affirmative commands (imperative mode) - Regular Verbs

In order to give a command such as "take a seat, please", "follow me", etc. we need to make some changes to the verbs that we use. This is a very simple process and the rule is very easy.

We must remember that in Spanish, verbs end in *AR*, *ER* or *IR*, for example: caminar (to walk), comer (to eat), escribir (to write); so we change the endings if we want to say a comand.

Study the following examples:

Verbs ending in	–ar	–er	-ir
Change ending to:			
Formal command:	-e	-a	-a
Informal command:	-a	-e	-e

Example:

	Esperar (to wait)	Comer (to eat)	Escribir (to write)
Formal command:	¡Espere!	¡Coma!	¡Escriba!
Informal command:	¡Espera!	¡Come!	¡Escribe!

Actividad F: Now you try it! Write the command form of the following verbs, by changing the infinitive form to the imperative form:

	llamar	bajar	subir	mirar
Formal command:				
Informal command:				

Asociaciones:
Dibuje una línea entre el vocabulario de columna A y el inglés de columna B.

A.

¿En qué le puedo servir?

Perdón.

Con permiso.

Gracias por su paciencia.

De nada.

por favor

Gracias

B.

Excuse me. (1)

You're welcome.

Thank you.

Thank you for your patience.

May I help you?

Excuse me(2)

please

Más Asociaciones:
Asocie los siguientes imperativos con las figuras. Todos los imperativos son formales.

1. ¡venga conmigo!

2. ¡escuche!

3. ¡siéntese!

4. ¡espere un momento!

5. ¡mire!

6. ¡vaya!

Nota Cultural: Los Hispanos in the United States

More than 37 million people in the United States, or more than one in eight persons, are of Hispanic origin. This population, representing 7.6 million households, ranks as the 5th largest Spanish-speaking group in the world. Approximately 70% of these *Hispanos* reside in 4 states, California, Texas, New York, and Florida. The majority of Spanish-speaking people in the United States are from Mexico, Puerto Rico, and Cuba. In the past 30 years, a large number of immigrants has also arrived from Central America and the Dominican Republic.

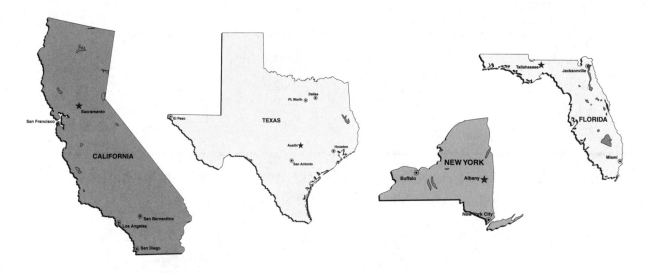

 Expresiones Útiles: Practique estas expresiones y úselas diariamente para aprenderlas bien. Escuche y repita:

A bit slower, please.	Un poco más despacio, por favor.
Can you repeat that?	¿Puede repetirlo?
Do you speak English?	¿Hablas inglés?
How do you say that in Spanish?	¿Cómo se dice esto en español?
I don't know.	No sé.
I don't mind.	No me importa.
I don't understand.	No comprendo.
Maybe	Quizás
What does this word mean?	¿Qué significa esta palabra?
How do you say it?	¿Cómo se dice?

Pronunciación: Las Vocales I, O and U

1. The Spanish **I** is always pronounced like the double **ee** in the English word **"see."**

   When the letter **y** stands alone or comes at the end of a word, it is also pronounced like the double **ee** just like the Spanish letter **I**. Otherwise, it is just like the English **y**.

   Escuche y repita: si mi linda misa cita

   Escuche y repita: muy rey soy doy

   Escuche y repita: yo ya yema yeso tuya

2. The Spanish **O** sounds like the English **o** in the word **no**…but it is short and clipped, not drawn out.

   Escuche y repita: No con son tomo coca-cola

3. The Spanish **U** is like the **oo** in the English word **moo**, but, again, short.

   Escuche y repita: luna cuna fumo bambú Lulú

Tarea (Homework):

1. Practice the dialogs at the beginning of the chapter.

2. Study the meanings and pronunciation of the vocabulary and useful expressions.

3. Try to give directions from your work area to another area in the building using the vocabulary from this chapter.

4. Look up 4 verbs in the dictionary. Practice forming and saying the command forms.

5. In situations requiring a courteous reply, say it in Spanish.

Vocabulario Lección 3:
Escuche y Repita.

Perdone.	Excuse me.
Muchas gracias.	Thanks a lot.
De nada.	You're welcome.
¿En qué le puedo servir?	May I help you?
por favor	please
Gracias por su paciencia.	Thank you for your patience.
Vaya derecho.	Go straight.
doble, vire	turn
Espere un momento.	Wait a minute.
¡Siéntese!	Sit down!
¡Venga conmigo!	Come with me!
¡Apúrese!	Hurry up! (formal)
¡Mira! ¡Mire!	Look! (formal)
¡Escucha! ¡Escuche!	Listen! (formal)
el restaurante	restaurant
estar	to be located/to feel
cerca/lejos (de)	close (to)/far(from)
aquí/allí	here/there
a la derecha	to the right
a la izquierda	to the left
al lado de	next to
el correo	post office
el gerente	the manager
ocupado/a	busy
después de	after
unos minutos	a few minutes
poder (ue)	to be able to
Yo puedo	I can
Tu puedes	You can
Él, ella, Ud. puede	He/she/you, formal can
hablar	to speak
con	with
ahora	now
hijo(a)	son(daughter)
Es tarde/temprano.	It's late/early.
bueno	OK
venir (irreg)	to come
Ya voy	I am coming

COMMUNICATION GOALS:	To talk about family members
	To describe people and things
	To describe location and position

STRUCTURE:	Descriptive Adjectives
	Possessive Adjectives
	Verbs Ser and Estar

| PRONUNCIATION: | The letters B and V |

| CULTURAL FOCUS: | Hispanic families and names |

¿Sabía Ud?

The Atacama Desert in **Chile** is the driest place on the earth, averaging only three hundredths of an inch of rain per year. The city of Calama, with 150,000 inhabitants located in the middle of the desert, has never recorded any precipitation. Ocean currents just off the Pacific coast keep clouds offshore, forcing most rain to fall into the ocean.

Conversación:
Escuche.

Diálogo 4.1

Pablo y Pedro hablan de sus familias.

Pablo: ¿Dónde vive tu familia?

Pedro: Mis padres viven aquí en California.

Pablo: ¿Tienes hermanos?

Pedro: Sí, tengo dos hermanos y una hermana.

Pablo: Yo también tengo dos hermanos. Tengo un hermano mayor y otro menor.

Diálogo 4.2

Rocío y Paula describen a sus familias.

Rocío: Paula, ¿Cómo es tu madre?

Paula: Mi madre es alta, delgada y simpática.

Rocío: ¿Cómo está tu padre?

Paula: Mi padre está muy ocupado. Trabaja mucho.

Rocío: ¿Cuántos años tiene tu padre?

Paula: Mi padre tiene 42 años. Y mi abuelo tiene 62 años. Él está muy contento. Está jubilado.

Diálogo 4.3

Joselito y su mamá hablan de su familia

Joselito: Mamá, ¿De dónde es tío Pío?

Mamá: Tío Pío es de México. Y tía María es de México, también. Ellos son mexicanos. Pero ahora están en Texas.

Joselito: ¿Y Luis y Luisa son sus hijos y mis primos, verdad?

Mamá: Claro, mijo*. Son tus primos. Son muy graciosos.

*The combination of the words "mi hijo" is an affectionate way to refer to one's son.

28

Actividad A: Escuche y repita: Escuche cada diálogo y repita.

Actividad B: En parejas, lea cada diálogo.

Actividad C: Preguntas personales: Conteste las siguientes preguntas.

1. ¿Dónde vive tu familia?

2. ¿Tienes hermanos? ¿Cuántos?

3. ¿Son tus hermanos mayores o menores?

4. ¿Cómo es tu padre?

5. ¿Cuántos años tiene tu abuela?

6. ¿Cómo es tu esposo(a)? ¿Cómo se llama él/ella?

7. ¿Tienes hijos? ¿Cuántos?

8. ¿Cómo se llama tu hijo(a)?

9. ¿De dónde eres? Y tus padres, ¿de dónde son?

10. ¿Cuántos primos tienes? ¿Muchos? ¿Pocos?

Actividad D: Los contrarios: Dibuje una línea entre la Columna A y la Columna B mostrando los contrarios.

A	B
1. mayor	antipático
2. alto	pequeño
3. joven	delgado
4. grande	bajo
5. malo	menor
6. mucho	feo
7. simpático	viejo
8. bonito	poco
9. gordo	bueno

Estructura: El verbo "SER"

The verb SER means "to be" in the sense of descriptions about a person, whether physically or intellectually.

Yo soy	I am
Tú eres	You are - informal
Él, ella es	He/she is
Ud. Es	You are - formal
Nosotros(as) somos	We are
Ellos/ellas son	They are
Uds. son	All of you are

Use "SER" plus an adjective to indicate characteristics or qualities inherent to a person. The following are some adjectives that are used with SER.

alto	tall		lindo	pretty
antipático	unpleasant		malo	bad
bajo	short		mayor	older
bonito	pretty		menor	younger
bueno	good		mucho	a lot
delgado	thin		pequeño	small
feo	ugly		pobre	poor
gordo	fat		poco	a little
grande	big		rico	rich
guapo	good-looking		simpático	pleasant
joven	young		viejo	old

Estructura: Adjetivos

Most adjectives that end in **o** have four possible forms, masculine, feminine, singular and plural, to agree with the noun or pronoun that they describe.

- Adjectives that end in **o** change **o** to **a** to modify a feminine singular noun or pronoun. Add **s** to form the plural adjective.

  Juan es alto. María es alta. Mis hermanos son altos.

- Adjectives that end in **e** or **a** in the masculine do not change in the feminine.

  Carlos es independiente. Marta es independiente.
  Raúl es deportista. Susana es deportista también.

- Most adjectives that end in a consonant in the masculine do not change in the feminine. Add *es* to form the plural adjective.

  Rico es popular. Julia es muy popular. Ellos son populares.

La posición de los adjetivos:

- In Spanish, descriptive adjectives generally come after the noun.

  Raúl es un hombre simpático.
  Cristina es una madre joven.

- "*Bueno*" and "*malo*" usually come before the noun. Before a masculine singular noun, "*bueno*" changes to "*buen*" and "*malo*" to "*mal*."

  Carlota es una buena hija. Y Carlitos es un buen hijo.
  Carlota no es una mala hija. Carlitos no es un mal hijo.

Actividad E: Descripciones: Haga una descripción de las siguientes personas. Use la forma correcta de SER + adjetivo para indicar características. Escoja de la lista.

¿Cómo es:

gracioso

perezoso

alto

bajo

bueno

malo

obediente

eficiente

maravilloso

fiel

difícil

fácil

rico

pobre

Ex. 1. ¿Tu mejor amigo(a)? Mi mejor amigo <u>es gracioso.</u>

2. ¿Tu esposo(a)?_____

3. ¿Tu hijo(a)?_____

4. ¿Tus hijos(as)?_____

5. ¿Tu gerente?_____

6. ¿Tu secretaria?_____

7. ¿Tu actor favorito?_____

8. ¿Tu profesor(a) de español?_____

9. ¿Tu perro/gato?_____

10. ¿Tu trabajo?_____

11. ¿Tu restaurante favorito?_____

Preguntas: Conteste las siguientes preguntas en frases completas. Use la forma correcta del verbo SER y un adjetivo. Compare sus respuestas con otro miembro de la clase.

1. ¿Cómo es Ud?   **Ex:** Yo <u>soy alto y elegante.</u>

2. ¿Cómo es tu jefe?   Mi jefe_____.

3. ¿Cómo es la secretaria en la oficina?   Ella_____.

4. ¿Cómo es el gerente de tu departamento?   Él_____.

Actividad F: Identifique los siguientes adjetivos. Dibuje una línea entre la palabra y el dibujo.

1. alto

2. delgado

3. guapo

4. pequeño

5. gordo

6. viejo

7. grande

8. feo

9. bonito

10. pobre

Estructura: El verbo "ESTAR"

The verb ESTAR means "to be" in the sense of how one feels or where one is located.

Yo estoy	I am
Tú estás	You are—informal
Él/ella está	He/she is
Ud. está	You are—formal
Nosotros(as) estamos	We are
Ellos/ellas están	They are
Uds. están	All of you are

Use "ESTAR" plus an adjective to indicate mental or physical condition at a given time. ESTAR is also used to indicate location. The following are adjectives used with ESTAR.

aburrido

loco

cansado

nervioso

contento

ocupado

enfermo

preocupado

enojado

triste

35

Actividad G: Conteste en español con frases completas

1. ¿Estás contento(a) con tu clase de español?
2. A veces (sometimes), ¿estás aburrido(a) con tu trabajo?
3. ¿Estás cansado(a)? ¿Trabajas mucho?
4. ¿Estás preocupado(a) por tu familia?
5. ¿Estás muy ocupado(a)? ¿Por qué?

Estructura: Los Adjetivos posesivos.

In Spanish, the possessive adjective written before the noun agrees with the thing possessed, not with the possessor. Let's read the following examples:

Mi padre	**Mis** padres	My
Tu abuelo	**Tus** abuelos	Your
Su hermana	**Sus** hermanas	His, her, its, your(formal)
Nuestro amigo		Our
Nuestra amiga		
Nuestros amigos		
Nuestras amigas		

Notice that all the possessive adjectives have singular and plural forms, which change depending on how many things are possessed. The possessive **nuestro** has singular and plural, as well as masculine and feminine forms; this is the only adjective with gender.

Actividad H: Use la forma correcta del adjectivo posesivo y la forma correcta del verbo ESTAR, para expresar con quien están cada una de estas personas.
Por ejemplo:

Ex: Marta: los amigos   Marta <u>está con</u> **sus** <u>amigos</u>.

1. Roberto: los hermanos_____

2. Ana: el padre_____

3. Rita: la amiga_____

4. Teresa y María: el primo_____

5. El Sr. Gómez: la esposa_____

6. nosotros: las primas_____

7. Yo: los abuelos_____

8. Tú: el padre_____

9. Pablo: los amigos_____

10. Yo: el perro_____

Actividad I: Entrevista: (an interview) Hable con un(a) compañero(a) de clase y hágale las preguntas y apunte la información.

Ex. 1. ¿De dónde eres?   Yo <u>soy de Ecuador</u>.

2. ¿Cómo estás hoy? Explique.   Yo_____.

3. ¿Dónde estás en este momento? Yo_____.

4. ¿Cómo eres?   Yo_____.

5. ¿Quién es una de tus personas favoritas? ¿Cómo es él/ella?

Una de mis personas favoritas es_____.

El/Ella es_____.

Nota Cultural: La Familia Hispana

Whether *tradicional* or modern, Hispanic families generally place great importance on family ties. The concept of family includes not only immediate family, but also aunts, uncles, cousins, grandparents, and godparents.

In many Hispanic families, parents, children, and grandparents often live in the same house. Grandparents play an important role in child rearing, often caring for them when parents are away. Sons and daughters commonly continue living at home until they marry.

Family celebrations of all kinds are important events in the Spanish-speaking world. Birthdays, baptisms, first communions, and weddings are joyous occasions celebrated with food and family.

Nombres Españoles

Spanish first names are usually given in honor of Catholic saints. Many girls' names refer to the Virgin Mary. In addition to birthdays, many Hispanics also celebrate their saint's day. This is the day on which the Catholic Church honors a particular saint. Some Hispanics are named after the saint being honored the day they were born.

When a Hispanic woman marries, she keeps her maiden name and adds her husband's last name to hers. For example, when María Delgado marries José Martínez, her name becomes María Delgado de Martínez. The children of José and María will have the last name Martínez Delgado.

Expresiones Útiles: Practique estas expresiones y úselas diariamente para aprenderlas bien. Escuche y Repita:

I'd like	Quisiera
Is there?	¿Hay?
It is	Es
There is	Hay
This is	Esto es
What is this?	¿Qué es esto?

Pronunciación: The Letters B and V

1. There is a slight difference between the Spanish B and V. The English V sound is not used in Spanish. If a word begins with either B or V, or after the letters m or n, use the B sound as in the English word boy. Por ejemplo:

   Repita: banana barba vote sombrero vámonos

2. Between two vowels, the sound is made with the lips barely touching. Start to say the letter b, but don't close your lips all of the way allowing air to pass through them. Por ejemplo:

   Repita: estuvo sabe llave nube rebelde

Tarea (Homework):

1. Practice the dialogs at the beginning of the chapter.

2. Study the meanings and pronunciation of the vocabulary and useful expressions.

3. Describe your family in Spanish. Tell who the person is and what the person is like. Tell how they are feeling right now. Use the correct possessive adjective and the correct form of the descriptive adjective. Use the correct form of the verbs SER and ESTAR.

4. Conjugate the verbs SER and ESTAR. (i.e. give all the subject pronouns with the matching form of the verb.)

Vocabulario Lección 4:
Escuche y Repita.

la familia	the family	joven	young
el padre	the father	bonito/lindo	pretty
la madre	the mother	feo	ugly
los padres	the parents	guapo	good-looking
el hijo	the son	grande	big
la hija	the daughter	pequeño	small
los hijos	the children	bueno	good
el hermano	the brother	malo	bad
la hermana	the sister	simpático	nice
los hermanos	the brothers and sisters	antipático	not nice
		mayor(es)	older
el esposo	the husband	menor(es)	younger
la esposa	the wife	mucho	a lot
el tío	the uncle	poco	a little (in amount)
la tía	the aunt	rico	rich
el primo/la prima	the cousin	pobre	poor
el abuelo	the grandfather	aburrido	bored
la abuela	the grandmother	cansado	tired
el hombre	the man	contento	happy
la mujer	the woman	enfermo	sick
mi/mis	my	enojado	angry
tu/tus	your	loco	crazy
su/sus	his, her, your (formal), their	nervioso	nervous
		ocupado	busy
nuestro(a)/ nuestros(as)	our	preocupado	worried
		triste	sad
alto*	tall	estar	to be (feelings/location)
bajo	short		
delgado	thin	ser	to be (physical characteristics)
gordo	fat		
viejo	old	maravilloso	awesome
eficiente	efficient	perezoso, vago	lazy
fiel	loyal, faithful	obediente	obedient

*Adjectives that end in the letter "o" change the **o** to "**a**" to form the feminine.

COMMUNICATION GOALS:	To identify office objects
	To indicate and ask for location
STRUCTURE:	Estar + location
	Prepositions
PRONUNCIATION:	Letters D and T
CULTURAL FOCUS:	Holidays

¿Sabía Ud?

Costa Rica, discovered by Christopher Columbus in 1502, was named "rich coast" for all of the natural resources found there. Costa Rica is home to numerous volcanoes, including Arenal, the second largest active volcano in the world. There are more Americans living in Costa Rica than Costa Ricans living in the United States.

Conversación:
Escuche.

Diálogo 5.1

Ana:	¿Dónde está Raúl?
Pepe:	Está en la cafetería.
Ana:	¿Y dónde está la cafetería?
Pepe:	Está a la derecha de la oficina.

Diálogo 5.2

Por teléfono: José llama a María. María no está en casa.

Miguel:	¡Diga!
José:	¿Aló? ¿Está María en casa?
Miguel:	No, no está en este momento.
José:	¿A qué hora regresa?
Miguel:	A las dos. Después del almuerzo.
José:	Gracias.
Miguel:	¡No hay de qué!

Diálogo 5.3

Una señorita pide direcciones.

Srta. Vargas:	¿Dónde está la oficina del gerente?
Secretaria:	La oficina del gerente está al lado de la recepción.
Srta. Vargas:	¿Está lejos de aquí?
Secretaria:	No, está cerca. Vaya por el pasillo y está a la izquierda, en frente de la cafetería, al lado de la recepción.
Srta. Vargas:	Gracias.
Secretaria:	De nada.

Actividad A: Escuche y repita: Escuche cada diálogo y repita.

Actividad B: En parejas, lea cada diálogo.

Actividad C: Identifique el vocabulario.

1. ¿Dónde están ellos?

2. ¿Dónde está la oficina?

3. ¿Dónde está la cafetería?

4. ¿Por dónde va Pedro?

5. ¿Dónde están los gerentes?

6. ¿A qué hora regresa Pablo?

Actividad D: Preguntas Personales.

1. ¿Dónde estás en este momento?

2. ¿Dónde está tu oficina?

3. ¿A qué hora comes el almuerzo?

4. ¿Quién está a tu lado en este momento?

5. Cuando estás en la cafetería, ¿qué hay a la izquierda? ¿Y a la derecha?

Estructura: Estar + Location
Remember from lección 4:

The verb **estar** is used to indicate where something or someone is located. It tells where the subject is.

Yo estoy	I am
Tú estás	You are - informal
Él, ella está	He/she is
Usted está	You are - formal
Nosotros(as) estamos	We are
Ellos/Ellas están	They are
Ustedes están	All of you are

Actividad E: Complete las oraciones con la forma correcta del verbo ESTAR.

1. Carlos _____ en México.

2. ¿Dónde _____ la cafetería?

3. Mis amigos _____ en la oficina.

4. Nosotros _____ en la recepción.

5. Yo no _____ en casa.

6. ¿Dónde _____ tú?

7. Marta e Irene _____ felices.

8. Elena, Marcos y yo _____ cansados.

9. La playa _____ muy lejos.

Estructura: Preposiciones

Prepositions help describe location. Some form of the verb estar + a preposition tells where someone or something is located.

Él está **entre** los camiones.

El auto está **delante** del* camión.

El camión está **detrás** del auto.

El camión verde está **al* lado del** camión azul.

El mecánico está **debajo** del camión.

El hombre está **encima** del camión.

El coche está **adentro**.

El coche está **afuera**.

*de before the word el contracts to del. De + el = del. De = of, from

*a before the word el contracts to al. A + el = al. A= to

45

Actividad F: Asociaciones: Dibuje una línea entre las preposiciones en las columnas A y B.

A	B

<table>
<tr><td>A</td><td>B</td></tr>
</table>

A

1. cerca de
2. lejos de
3. a la izquierda
4. a la derecha
5. adentro
6. afuera
7. al lado de
8. frente de
9. debajo de
10. encima de
11. entre
12. detrás de
13. delante de

B

close to

behind

far from

next to

to the left of

inside

on top of

in front of

outside

between

underneath

to the right

across from

Actividad G: Escuche y Repita. Vocabulario de la oficina.

El escritorio

La ventana

La silla

El reloj

El papel

El ordenador/la computadora

El libro

La impresora

La pluma

El ratón

El lápiz

La papelera/la basura

El cuaderno

El archivo

El calendario

La calculadora

El mapa

La grapadora

La luz

Las tijeras

La pared

La cinta adhesiva

La puerta

El tablero de anuncios

Actividad H: ¿Dónde está? Use el vocabulario nuevo y las preposiciones para decir dónde están las siguientas cosas y personas.

1.

la secretaria

2.

la silla

3.

el hombre

4.

la grapadora

5.

los papeles

6.

las plumas

 Expresiones Útiles: Practique estas expresiones. Escuche y Repita:

Don't worry.	No se preocupe.
Good idea.	Buena idea.
I think so.	Creo qué sí.
Maybe	Quizás
More or less	Más or menos
That depends.	Depende.

Nota Cultural: Feriados

Spanish speaking countries celebrate religious and civic holidays, just as we do in this country. The religious holidays have their origin in Catholicism and civic holidays celebrate historical happenings. In Central and South America, many religious festivals still retain elements of pre-Colombian native practices.

While each Spanish-speaking country has individual celebrations, many countries have holidays in common. Among the most popular is Semana Santa, or Holy Week. During this solemn, religious celebration, people parade through the streets carrying floats representing Christ, his mother Mary, and biblical scenes. Music, dancing, and fireworks conclude Holy Week activities.

The fiesta of San Fermín in Pamplona, Spain lasts 9 days. Celebrating a city's patron saint is common in Spanish-speaking countries. San Fermín, the patron saint of Pamplona's bakers, wine merchants, and wine-skin makers, was martyred in the 3rd century A.D. This festival is noteworthy for the famous "running of the bulls" through the streets of Pamplona. Hotel reservations for this holiday are made a year in advance. Bands play all night while participants drink and party the night away.

In Mexico, the feast of the Virgin of Guadalupe is another religious holiday. Celebrated annually on December 12 since 1531, an estimated 10 million people visit the main Basilica in Mexico City, making it the most visited Catholic church in the world after the Vatican. As the Virgin of Guadalupe is Mexico's patron saint, pilgrims seeking her intercession often travel many days before arriving at the Basilica's main altar. Many miracles, cures, and interventions have been attributed to the Virgin.

Civic celebrations across Latin America remember independence days. Cities decorated with flags, politicians making appearances, parades, beauty queens, dances, fireworks, and parks filled with families enjoying the day together all serve to commemorate the event.

Pronunciación: The Letters T and D

1. When you say the letter **T** in English, a slight puff of air leaves your mouth. The Spanish **T** does not have that breath following it. Put your tongue behind your top teeth and make sure that you don't feel any air come out of your mouth. (Put your hand in front of your mouth and say **Tom**. Did you feel a puff of air hit your hand? You should have. Now do it again, but this time say **Tomás**…no air should hit your hand, if you said it correctly.)

   Repita: tonto tía teléfono santo tiempo

2. The letter **D** is pronounced in several different ways depending on its position in the word. Between 2 vowels, it is pronounced like the **th** sound in the English word "mother."

   Repita: nada adiós todo estado tímido

3. At the beginning of a word, or after the letters **N** and **L**, the **D** is pronounced like the English word "dot."

   Repita: banda cuándo dónde dentista doctor

   At the end of a word, the **D** is pronounced like a soft **th** sound.

   Repita: libertad universidad ciudad verdad bondad

Tarea:

1. Practice the dialogs at the beginning of the chapter.

2. Study the meanings and pronunciation of the vocabulary and useful expressions.

3. Make vocabulary cards with the prepositions listed on one side in Spanish and the other in English. Flip through the cards for practice.

4. Identify things in your home office or at work in Spanish. Tell where each item is located.

Vocabulario Lección 5:
Escuche y Repita.

la cafetería	cafeteria	la engrapadora	stapler
la oficina	office	las tijeras	scissors
la recepción	front desk	el pegamento	glue
el pasillo	hallway	la regla	ruler
el almuerzo	lunch	la cinta adhesiva	tape
el gerente	manager	¡diga!	Hello (when answering phone)
el conductor	driver		
el coche	car	en casa	at home
el camión	truck	rojo	red
el mecánico	mechanic	azul	blue
el escritorio	desk	a la derecha	to the right
la silla	chair	a la izquierda	to the left
el papel	paper	al lado de	next to
el libro	book	al otro lado de	on the other side of
el bolígrafo	pen	lejos de	far from
el lápiz	pencil	cerca de	close to
el cuaderno	notebook	aquí	here
el calendario	calendar	allí	there
el mapa	map	dentro de	inside of
la luz	light	fuera de	outside of
la pared	wall	con	with
la puerta	door	sin	without
la ventana	window	afuera	outside
el reloj	clock, watch	adentro	inside
el ordenador/		encima de	on top of
la computadora	computer	debajo de	underneath
la impresora	printer	detrás de	behind
el ratón	mouse	delante de	in front of
la papelera/		entre	between
la basura	trash can	en	in/on
el archivo	file	frente de	across from
la calculadora	calculator		

COMMUNICATION GOALS:	To ask and respond to yes and no questions To ask questions To indicate dates and days of the week To describe weather and the seasons
STRUCTURE:	Interrogatives Affirmative and Negative questions and answers Days, months, seasons Hacer to express weather
PRONUNCIATION:	"QU"
CULTURAL FOCUS:	Pasatiempos – Leisure time activities

¿Sabía Ud?

El Salvador is the smallest, yet most populated country in Central America. About the size of the state of Massachusetts, it is the only Central American country not bordering the Caribbean Sea. Although called the land of volcanoes, devastating earthquakes have been responsible for extensive destruction in El Salvador as recently as 2001.

Conversación:

Escuche.

Diálogo 6.1

Mariana y Clara trabajan en la misma oficina.

Mariana:	¿Qué día es hoy?
Clara:	Hoy es lunes.
Mariana:	¿Y cuál es la fecha de hoy?
Clara:	Hoy es el 7 de junio.
Mariana:	¿Cuándo es tu cumpleaños?
Clara:	Es mañana. El 8 de junio.
Mariana:	¡Feliz Cumpleaños!

Diálogo 6.2

Beto y Linda toman café en la cocina. Linda lee el periódico.

Beto:	¿Qué tiempo hace?
Linda:	Hace sol.
Beto:	¿Hace mucho sol?
Linda:	Sí, ¡hace sol y mucho calor!
Beto:	¡Qué bueno!
Linda:	¿Por qué?
Beto:	Porque hoy es el picnic de la compañía. Muchos empleados van al parque Marín para celebrar el éxito del departamento de mercadeo.
Linda:	¡Qué divertido!

Diálogo 6.3

En una fiesta de la compañía Rey:

Manuel:	¿Quién es el hombre al lado de Pablo?
Rubén:	¿El hombre alto y rubio?
Manuel:	Sí.
Rubén:	Es Alberto Martín.
Manuel:	¿Es el nuevo gerente del departamento de contabilidad?
Rubén:	No, es el director de Recursos Humanos.
Manuel:	¿Cómo es él?
Rubén:	Él es simpático y muy trabajador.

Actividad A: Escuche y repita: Escuche y repita cada diálogo.

Actividad B: En parejas, lea cada diálogo.

Actividad C: Preguntas. Conteste las preguntas según los diálogos.

Diálogo 1:

    1. ¿Quienes participan en esta conversación?

    2. ¿Cuál es la fecha de hoy?

    3. ¿Cuándo es el cumpleaños de Clara?

Diálogo 2:

    1. ¿Qué tiempo hace?

    2. ¿Hace frío también?

    3. ¿A dónde va Beto hoy? ¿Por qué?

Diálogo 3:

    1. ¿Quién es Alberto Martín?

    2. ¿Cómo es él?

    3. ¿Cuál es su profesión?

Actividad D: Aprendamos los días de la semana y los meses del año.
Escuche y repita:

Días de la semana	Days of the week
lunes	Monday
martes	Tuesday
miércoles	Wednesday
jueves	Thursday
viernes	Friday
sábado	Saturday
domingo	Sunday

Meses del año	Months of the year
enero	January
febrero	February
marzo	March
abril	April
mayo	May
junio	June
julio	July
agosto	August
septiembre	September
octubre	October
noviembre	November
diciembre	December

Preguntas:

1. ¿En qué mes es tu cumpleaños?
2. ¿En qué mes es navidad?
3. ¿En qué mes celebramos la independencia de los Estados Unidos?
4. ¿Cuál es el primer mes del año?
5. ¿Cuál es tu mes favorito?
6. ¿En qué mes es su aniversario de bodas?
7. ¿Qué días trabaja usted en la empresa?
8. ¿En qué días no trabaja?
9. ¿Cuándo sale de vacaciones?
10. ¿En qué mes nació su primer hijo?

*Remember that days of the week and months are not capitalized in Spanish.

Actividad E: Vocabulario: Escuche y Repita.

Diciembre

lunes	martes	miércoles	jueves	viernes	sábado	domingo
	1 **Fiesta**	2	3	4	5	6
7	8	9	10	11	12	13
14	15	16 *Cumpleaños*	17	18	19	20
21	22	23	24	25 **Navidad**	26	27
28	29	30	31			

Preguntas: El calendario:

1. ¿Qué día de la semana es el 5 de diciembre?

2. ¿Cuándo es el 22 de diciembre?

3. ¿Cuántas semanas hay en diciembre?

4. ¿Cuándo es la fiesta de cumpleaños? ¿Y qué día?

Actividad F: El tiempo. ¿Qué tiempo hace? Escuche y repita.

1. Hace buen tiempo.
2. Hace mal tiempo.
3. Hace calor.
4. Hace frío.
5. Hace sol.
6. Hace fresco.
7. Está nublado.
8. Llueve.
9. Nieva.
10. Hace viento.

The verb **HACER** is used in Spanish to express most, but not all, weather conditions.

Preguntas:

1.   ¿Qué tiempo hace hoy?

2.   ¿En qué meses hace mucho calor?

3.   ¿Hace calor en Alaska en noviembre?

4.   ¿Hace viento hoy?

Actividad G: Las Estaciones*: Escuche y repita.

| el verano | el invierno. | el otoño | la primavera |

*The seasons of the year are reversed in the northern and southern hemispheres. For example, when it is winter in Argentina, it is summer in the United States.

Identifique: Describa el tiempo en estos lugares.

1. ¿Qué tiempo hace en Las Vegas?

_____

3. ¿Qué tiempo hace en Alaska?

_____

2. ¿Qué estación es?

_____

4. ¿Qué estación es?

_____

5. ¿Qué tiempo hace en Florida?

_____

7. ¿Qué tiempo hace en el Caribe?

_____

6. ¿Qué estación es?

_____

8. ¿Qué estación es?

_____

Estructura: Preguntas de Sí y No.

When asking a "yes/no" question in Spanish, the subject can precede or follow the verb or sometimes be put at the very end of the sentence. An upside down question mark indicates where the question begins. Always raise your voice at the end of a question:

¿**Miércoles** <u>es</u> tu cumpleaños?	Wednesday is your birthday?
¿<u>Es</u> **miércoles** tu cumpleaños?	Is Wednesday your birthday?
¿<u>Es</u> tu cumpleaños **miércoles**?	Is your birthday Wednesday?

To answer a yes/no question affirmatively, put "Sí" before the statement.

Sí, mi cumpleaños es miércoles.   Yes, my birthday is Wednesday.

To answer negatively, use "no" twice. Once before the statement and again before the verb.

No, mi cumpleaños **no** es miércoles.   No, my birthday is not Wednesday.

Actividad H: Conteste Sí o No. Si contesta no, dé la información correcta.

1. ¿Hace mucho frío en el invierno?

2. ¿Es fácil aprender español?

3. ¿Tienes 10 años con tu empresa?

4. ¿Estás contento con tu trabajo?

5. ¿México está al norte de los Estados Unidos?

Actividad I: Frases Revueltas: Ponga las palabras en el orden correcto para hacer una pregunta. Recuerde que el orden del sujeto puede cambiarse.

Ex. 1. ¿Tu cumpleaños en febrero es? <u>¿Es tu cumpleaños en febrero?</u>

2. ¿de tu compañía Antonio Martín el presidente es? _____

3. ¿La oficina cerca de aquí está de la secretaria? _____

4. ¿María su nombre es? _____

5. ¿de la recepción frente la cafetería está? _____

Estructura: Palabras interrogativas.

¿Qué?	What?	¿Quién/quiénes?	Who?
¿Por qué?	Why?	¿Cuál/cuáles?	Which?
¿Cuándo?	When?	¿Cuánto?	How much?
¿Dónde?	Where?	¿Cuántos(as)?	How many?
¿Cómo?	How?		

NOTICE: All interrogative words have accent marks. The interrogative question word "quién" has a plural form, "quiénes," which we use when we are pretty sure the answer will be plural. The same is true for "cuál" and "cuáles."

Actividad J: Palabras interrogativas: Asociaciones: Escriba el número de la palabra interrogativa al lado del resto de la pregunta.

1. ¿Qué   _____ es la fecha de hoy?

2. ¿Por qué   _____ es el aniversario de la compañía?

3. ¿Cuándo   _____ está la oficina del presidente?

4. ¿Dónde   _____ es el gerente de la compañía?

5. ¿Cómo   _____ cuesta una coca-cola?

6. ¿Quién   _____ es tu trabajo?

7. ¿Quiénes   _____ día es hoy?

8. ¿Cuál   _____ trabajas en esta empresa?

9. ¿Cuánto   _____ estudiantes hay en la clase?

10. ¿Cuántos   _____ son los empleados del departamento de operaciones?

(¿Puedes contestar estas preguntas?)

Nota Cultural: Leisure Time and Sports

Sports are as popular in Hispanic countries as they are in the United States. There is a wide variety of favorite sports from country to country. While soccer, *el futbol*, is the most popular, baseball, basketball, and volleyball are also played. Baseball is especially popular in the Caribbean and Venezuela. Many major league players in the United States come from Spanish speaking countries.

Participating and watching sports are not the only leisure activities. Throughout the Americas, people love to visit and socialize with friends and family. Outings to festivals, picnics, and local carnivals are common weekend activities. Watching TV, going to the movies, or attending cultural events all add to the enjoyment of leisure time.

Parks and plazas fill with families on weekends. Tables are set up for long games of checkers and dominoes among the men, while women sit and chat and youngsters play. Whatever the activity, leisure time is time spent with family and friends.

Expresiones Útiles: Escuche y repita.

How may I help you?	¿En qué le puedo servir?
How do you say…in Spanish?	¿Cómo se dice … en español?
May I?	¿Se puede?
What does this mean?	¿Qué quiere decir esto?
What is this?	¿Qué es ésto?
What do you need?	¿Qué necesita?

Pronunciación: La letra "qu"

1. The letter "q" occurs only in combination with "qué" and "qui" which have a silent "u". "Qu" is just like the English "K". Escuche y repita.

    Qué quién aquí queso Quito

Tarea:

1. Practice the dialogs at the beginning of the chapter.

2. Study the meanings and pronounciation of the vocabulary and useful expressions.

3. Think about your job. Review the interrogatives and answer these questions:

    1. ¿Con quién trabajas?

    2. ¿Qué haces?

    3. ¿Cuál es tu profesión?

    4. ¿Dónde trabajas?

    5. ¿Cuándo trabajas?

    6. ¿Por qué trabajas?

4. There are nine interrogatives. Copy them carefully on a piece of paper. Write them in Spanish in a column. Next to them in column 2, write the English translation. Now fold the paper so that only column 2 is visible. Can you write the Spanish translation of the question words in column 3? After you do this, unfold your paper and look in column 1 to check your answers. Continue to do this exercise across the paper., showing only one column at a time. Always check your work.

Vocabulario Lección 6:
Escuche y Repita.

Los días de la semana	**The days of the week**
lunes	Monday
martes	Tuesday
miércoles	Wednesday
jueves	Thursday
viernes	Friday
sábado	Saturday
domingo	Sunday
hoy	today
mañana	tomorrow

Los meses del año	**The months of the year**
enero	January
febrero	February
marzo	March
abril	April
mayo	May
junio	June
julio	July
agosto	August
septiembre	September
octubre	October
noviembre	November
diciembre	December
el calendario	the calendar

Las estaciones	**The seasons**
el verano	summer
el otoño	fall (autumn)
el invierno	winter
la primavera	spring

Interrogativas	**Question words**
¿Quién/quiénes?	Who?
¿Qué?	What?

¿Cuándo?	When?
¿Dónde?	Where?
¿Cómo?	How?
¿Por qué?	Why?
¿Cuánto?	How much?
¿Cuántos(as)?	How many?
¿Cuál/cuáles?	Which?

El tiempo	**The weather**
Hace buen tiempo.	It's nice outside.
Hace mal tiempo.	It's bad weather.
Hace (mucho) calor.	It's (very) hot.
Hace frío.	It's cold.
Hace sol.	It's sunny.
Hace fresco.	It's cool.
Hace viento.	It's windy.
Está (muy) nublado.	It's (very) cloudy.
Hay nubes.	There are clouds.
Llueve.	It's raining.
Está lloviendo.	It's raining right now.
Nieva.	It's snowing.
Está nevando.	It's snowing right now.

¡Feliz Cumpleaños!	Happy birthday!
el picnic	the picnic
la compañía	the company
el parque	the park
los empleados	the employees
celebrar	to celebrate
el éxito	the success
el departamento del mercadeo	the marketing department
el gerente	the manager
Contabilidad	Accounting
Recursos Humanos	Human Resources

COMMUNICATION GOALS:	To identify parts of the body To describe ailments To make suggestions
STRUCTURE:	Vamos + a + infinitive Por qué no + nosotros form of the verb Verbs doler and sentirse Body parts
PRONUNCIATION:	The letter R
CULTURAL FOCUS:	Curanderos

¿Sabía Ud?

Worldwide, Spanish is identified as the native language of 330 million people and the official language in 21 countries. Another 100 million use Spanish as a second language. In the United States, 13% of the population (nearly 35 million people) speak Spanish as their first language. Spanish ranks second around the world as a language for international communication and third in terms of international political, economic, and cultural language.

Conversación

Escuche.

Diálogo 7.1

Jorge Borges está enfermo hoy. No puede ir a su trabajo. Él llama a su supervisor para reportarse enfermo.

Secretaria:	¿Aló? Johnson e Hijos. ¿En qué le puedo servir?
Jorge:	Hola, muy buenos días. Soy Jorge Borges. No puedo ir hoy a trabajar, no me siento bien.
Secretaria:	Bueno, Sr. Borges. ¿En qué departamento trabaja usted?
Jorge:	En el departamento de transporte.
Secretaria:	¿Y cual es su número de identificación?
Jorge:	77-12574
Secretaria:	Gracias. Qué se mejore pronto. Adiós.
Jorge:	Gracias. Adiós.

Diálogo 7.2

Jorge va a la clínica. Todavía no se siente bien. Jorge habla con el doctor Chuy.

El médico:	Buenos días, Sr. Borges. ¿Qué le pasa?
Jorge:	No me siento bien. Me duele el estómago y también tengo dolor de cabeza.
El médico:	¿Cuánto tiempo hace que se siente mal?
Jorge	Hace 2 días.
El médico:	Ud. necesita antibióticos. También, debe descansar y tomar mucho jugo.
Jorge:	Gracias, doctor Chuy.

Diálogo 7.3

Paco se lastimó la cabeza. Tiene que llenar un informe de accidente.

El gerente:	Hola, Paco. ¿Qué tienes?
Paco:	Me siento mal. Me duele la cabeza. Me lastimé en el almacén hace 2 días.
El gerente:	¿Por qué no vamos a la enfermería y llenamos un informe de accidente? ¿Qué te parece?
Paco:	Bueno, vamos.

Actividad A: Escuche y repita: Escuche cada diálogo y repita.

Actividad B: En parejas, lea cada diálogo.

Actividad C: Escuche y repita: El cuerpo humano:

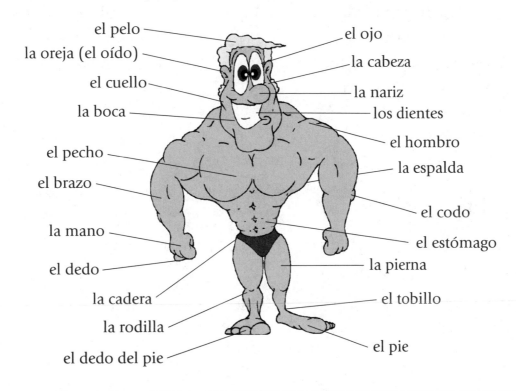

el pelo
la oreja (el oído)
el cuello
la boca
el pecho
el brazo
la mano
el dedo
la cadera
la rodilla
el dedo del pie

el ojo
la cabeza
la nariz
los dientes
el hombro
la espalda
el codo
el estómago
la pierna
el tobillo
el pie

Actividad D: ¿Qué le duele? Indique el parte del cuerpo que le duele.
Ex: **¿Qué le duele? Me duele(n) _el pie._**

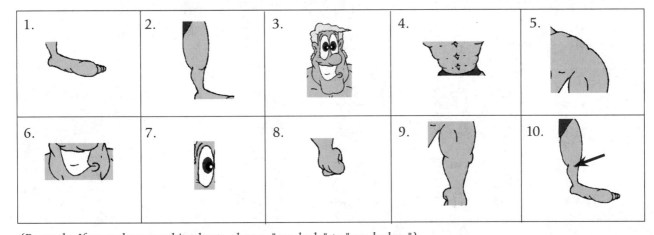

1.	2.	3.	4.	5.
6.	7.	8.	9.	10.

(Recuerde: If more than one thing hurts, change "me duele" to "me duelen.")

69

Actividad E: Asociaciones: ¿Puede asociar las expresiones de la columna A con el inglés de la columna B?

1. ¿Qué le pasa?	_____ I have a fever.
2. ¿Le duele algo?	_____ My leg is broken.
3. Tengo fiebre.	_____ Do you have health insurance?
4. Necesito una ambulancia.	_____ Should I call a doctor?
5. ¿Tiene ud. seguro médico?	_____ Does something hurt you?
6. Tengo rota la pierna.	_____ Can you breathe?
7. ¿Necesitas una silla de ruedas?	_____ I need an ambulance.
8. ¿Debo llamar al médico?	_____ Do you need a wheelchair?
9. ¿Puedes respirar?	_____ I feel better.
10. Me siento mejor.	_____ What's wrong with you?

Estructura:

1. We use the verbs *doler* and *sentirse* to express pain or ailments. Commonly used expressions include:

    Me duele + "part of the body" to indicate that something hurts
    Me duele**n**   to indicate that more than one thing hurts

2. To ask the question, **What hurts?**, we say:

    ¿Qué te duele? (informal)   ¿Qué le duele? (formal)

    Both questions would be answered: Me duele(n)….

3. To express how we feel, we use the verb **sentirse** (a reflexive verb). We say:

    Me siento + "adjective"

    Examples:
    Me siento bien.   I feel fine.   Me siento mal.   I feel bad.
    Me siento mejor.   I feel better.   ¡Me siento fantástico!   I feel fantastic!

4. To ask someone how they are feeling, we say:

    ¿Cómo te sientes? (informal)   ¿Cómo se siente usted? (formal)

    Both questions would be answered: Me siento + "adjective"

Actividad F: Situaciones. Lea la conversación. Luego, cambie las partes <u>subrayadas</u> (underlined).

<u>Diálogo 7.4</u>

Jorge llama por teléfono para reportarse enfermo.

A: Buenos días. Me llamo <u>Jorge Borges.</u> No iré a trabajar.

B: ¿Por qué no?

A: Me siento mal. Me duele <u>la cabeza.</u> (el estómago)

B: Bueno, ¿en qué <u>departamento</u> trabaja? (oficina)

A: En <u>transporte.</u> (contabilidad)

B: Y su <u>supervisor</u>, ¿quién es? (gerente, jefe)

A: Es <u>la señora Rodríguez.</u> (el señor Pérez)

B: Gracias, <u>Jorge.</u> ¡Qué se mejore pronto!

A: Adiós.

<u>Diálogo 7.5</u>

(En el consultorio médico)

A: Buenos días. <u>¿Cómo te sientes</u> hoy?

B: No muy bien.

A: <u>¿Qué te duele</u>?

B: Me duele <u>el brazo.</u>

A: ¿Cuánto tiempo hace que te duele?

B: Hace <u>2 días</u> (semanas/meses/horas).

A: ¡Ay, caramba! Debes tomar <u>2 aspirinas</u> cada 4 horas y
    debes <u>dormir</u> mucho también.

<u>Diálogo 7.6</u>

(En la oficina)

A: No puedo <u>usar la computadora.</u>

B: ¿Por qué no? ¿Qué pasa?

A: ¡Me siento fatal! Me duelen <u>los ojos.</u>

B: ¡Qué barbaridad! ¡Debes <u>descansar</u>!

A: ¡Buena idea!

B: ¡Que te mejores pronto!

Actividad G: Usando las fotos y la lista de vocabulario, describa cómo se sienten estas personas.

¿Como se siente(n)…

1. …Pedro y Carlos?

2. …su hermano?

3. …Francisco?

4. …mi jefe?

5. …Camilo?

6. …Alberto?

7. …Paco?

feliz   perezoso(a)   triste   enfermo(a)

cansado(a)   enojado(a)   bien

Actividad H: Práctica Oral. Exprese en español la siguiente situación:

Tell us about Maria. She has called in sick.   She had an emergency. She injured her arm and her head. She will use a cast for 2 weeks.

Estructura: Making suggestions.

Rather than telling employees or customers what to do, it is often more advantageous to suggest a solution to a problem. In Spanish, to make a suggestion, we simply ask: "Why don't we"....and follow that suggestion with the question, What do you think? Look at the examples:

¿Por qué no **hablamos** con el gerente? ¿Qué le parece?

Why don't we speak with the manager? What do you think?

¿Por qué no **llamamos** a la recepción? ¿Qué te parece?

Why don't we call the front desk? What do you think?

¿Por qué no **esperamos** aquí un momento? ¿Qué te parece?

Why don't we wait here for a minute? What do you think?

In each instance, to express "why don't we" the nosotros form of the verb was used.

The nosotros (we) form of the verb is formed by dropping the **ar, er** or **ir** of the infinitive and adding "**amos**," "**emos**,"and "**imos**," respectively. Study the examples:

Infinitive	Stem	"Nosotros" form
Hab**lar**	Habl	Habl**amos**
Com**er**	Com	Com**emos**
Escrib**ir**	Escrib	Escrib**imos**

Actividad I: Making a suggestion

¿Como se dice en español?

Ex. 1. ¿Por qué no  _____llamamos_____ al médico?

2. ¿Por qué no  _____en la cafetería?

3. ¿Por qué no  _____al gerente?

4. ¿Por qué no _____la medicina ahora?

5. ¿Por qué no _____ el libro?

6. ¿Por qué no  _____ mañana?

Nota Cultural: Curanderos

Since pre-hispanic times, *Curanderos* have been an important part of medicine in Mexico. The term comes from the word *curar*, meaning to heal. These contemporary spiritual and folk healers are the inheritors of a Native American shaman legacy, using herbal and folk remedies to treat both body and soul. Away from more urbanized areas, they remain a colorful part of Mexico's folk heritage.

Curanderos offer herbal and folk remedies as an economical source of heath care. In areas where people can not afford licensed doctors, hospitals, and pharmacies, the ancient practices often draw more clients than their modern counterparts. There, herbal medicines and other folk treatments are used with the confidence that North Americans use aspirin.

In the United States, many latino barrios feature *botánicas*, shops where healing herbs can be purchased. Continuing a long-standing tradition, barrio residents often use something other than prescription medication because of the herbs' familiarity, known effectiveness, and lesser cost. *Curanderos* are now being recognized for their intrinsic worth, taking their place along with a variety of alternative medical practices such as chiropractic, accupuncture, Chinese medicine, and naturopathy. Modern medicine has acknowledged the botanical tradition and uses many of the old cures, including chamomile tea for indigestion, *Amica* (mountain tobacco) to relieve sore muscles, *Raiz de valeriana* (Valerian root) as a headache remedy, and various herbal poultices to treat congestion.

 Expresiones Útiles: Practique estas expresiones y úselas para aprenderlas bien. Escuche y repita:

How do you feel?	¿Cómo te sientes?	I hurt my...	Me lastimé...
I feel...	Me siento...	leg	la pierna
dizzy	mareado(a)	arm	el brazo
faint	debilitado(a)	back	la espalda
poorly	mal	finger	el dedo
sick	enfermo(a)	knee	la rodilla
tired	cansado(a)		

Pronunciación: "R"

1. The letter **R** in Spanish, if not at the beginning of the word, sounds much like the English "tt" as in bitter, better, butter. Repeat those 3 words as quickly as you can to approximate the trill sound of the letter **R**.

   Escuche y repita: toro moro cara para pero

2. The initial **R** or **RR** has a rolled sound. Bounce your tongue against the roof of your mouth 2 or 3 times giving the effect of a trill sound.

   Escuche y repita: Roberto rata reina radio ridiculo Otra vez: perro carro corro cierro correcto

Tarea:

1. Practice the dialogs at the beginning of the chapter.

2. Study the meanings and pronounciation of the vocabulary and useful expressions.

3. With a small group, play "Simon dice." Simon says!

   Simon dice toque la cabeza. Simon says touch your head. Simon says so we can do it. Toque la mano. Touch your hand. This we don't do because Simon did not give the command. Practice parts of the body with this game.

4. Pretend that you and your partner are both hypocondriacs. You meet in a doctor's office. Discuss your ailments, recommend remedies and close the conversation by telling the other person to feel better soon. Use as much vocabulary from this chapter as you can.

Vocabulario Lección 7:
Escuche y Repita.

las partes del cuerpo humano:	**the parts of the human body:**
el ojo	eye
el pelo	hair
la cabeza	head
la nariz	nose
la boca	mouth
la garganta	throat
el cuello	neck
el corazón	heart
el brazo	arm
la muñeca	wrist
el dedo	finger
el estómago	stomach
la cadera	hip
el muslo	thigh
la rodilla	knee
el tobillo	ankle
el dedo del pie	toe
el pie	foot
la pierna	leg
la mano	hand
la espalda	back
el codo	elbow
el pecho	chest
el hombro	shoulder
los labios	lips
la oreja	ear
el oído	inner ear
los dientes	teeth

las enfermedades: **illnesses:**

Tengo fiebre.   I have a fever.
     tos.   a cough.
     gripe.   the flu.
     un resfriado.   a cold.
     una quémadura.   a burn.
     dolor de cabeza.   a headache.
     dolor de estómago.   a stomachache.
     dolor de garganta.   a sore throat.

expresiones: **expressions:**
¿Qué le parece a usted?   What do you think?
(¿Qué te parece? - informal)

¿Tienes (Tiene usted) seguro médico?	Do you have health insurance?
¿Cómo te sientes?	How do you feel? - informal
¿Cómo se siente usted?	How do you feel? - formal
Me siento…	I feel…
¿Qué te duele?	What hurts? - informal
¿Qué le duele a usted?	What hurts? - formal
Me duele(n)…	…hurts.
Me lastimé…	I hurt my…
¿Qué tienes?	What's wrong? - informal
¿Qué tiene usted?	What's wrong? - formal
deber	should/ought to
¿Cuánto tiempo hace qué…	How long has it been…?
Hace…	It's been….
descansar	to rest
sentarse	to sit down
beber	to drink
tomar	to take

Sustantivos:	Nouns:
el médico	doctor
la ambulancia	ambulance
la camilla	stretcher
una silla de ruedas	a wheelchair
la enfermera	nurse
la clínica	clinic
el hospital	hospital
la sala de espera	waiting room
una venda	bandage
la medicina	medicine
las pastillas	pills
el antibiótico	antibiotic
una inyección	injection
mejor/peor	better/worse
las muletas	crutches
la aspirina	aspirin
la sangre	blood

COMMUNICATION GOALS:	To talk about food
	To express likes/dislikes/preferences
	To make future plans
STRUCTURE:	Verbs gustar, preferir
	Ir + A + Infinitive
PRONUNCIATION:	H, LL, N
CULTURAL FOCUS:	Comida española

¿Sabía Ud?

We call it Basque Country, or *el País Vasco* in Spanish, but the Basque people call their land Euskadi. The Basques are an ancient ethnic group, existing since the Stone Age and retaining distinctive DNA traits. Basque Country is located in the folded hills of northern Spain along the Bay of Biscay. Largely untouched by Roman and Moorish invasions, the Basques have preserved a unique language unconnected to any known linguistic group.

Conversación:
Escuche.

Diálogo 8.1 En la cafetería

Pepe y Josefina comen en la cafetería de la compañía. Ellos trabajan en la misma oficina. Es mediodía.

Pepe: ¿Qué te gustaría comer?

Josefina: Me gustaría comer una ensalada de fruta y una hamburguesa con queso. ¿Y tú?

Pepe: Bueno, prefiero sopa, una ensalada y una hambuguesa.

Diálogo 8.2 En el restaurante

La señora Martín pide postre en un restaurante.

Camarero: ¿Desea más?

La señora M.: ¿Qué hay de postre?

Camarero: ¿De postre? A ver…tenemos helado, pastel o también fruta.

La señora M.: Me gustaría un pastel con café.

Camarero: ¿Café solo?

La señora M.: Sí, gracias.

Camarero: Ahora mismo, señora.

Diálogo 8.3 En el teléfono

María Lopez, la gerente de operaciones, y Esteban Morales, el agente comprador hablan por teléfono.

María: ¿Qué vas a hacer esta noche, Esteban?

Esteban: Voy a ir al restaurante Jalisco con James White, el representante de ventas de la compañía Johnson Brothers. ¿Te gustaría ir?

María: Un momento. Tengo que revisar mi horario… Bueno, ¿a qué hora van a salir ustedes?

Esteban: Vamos a salir a eso de las 7:00. Vamos a hablar un poco de la política de distribución y otros asuntos de negocios antes de comer.

María: Buena idea. Los encuentro en el restaurante entonces. Adiós.

Esteban: Hasta luego.

Actividad A: Escuche y repita: Escuche y repita cada diálogo.

Actividad B: En parejas, lea cada diálogo.

Actividad C: Verdadero o Falso: Según las conversaciones, indique si las siguientes oraciones son verdaderas o falsas.

Diálogo 1

1. Pepe y Josefina están en un restaurante elegante.
2. Ellos comen el almuerzo.
3. Pepe prefiere sopa con una hamburguesa y una ensalada.
4. Son las doce.
5. Josefina prefiere sólo una hamburguesa.

Diálogo 2

1. La señora Martín acaba de entrar en el restaurante.
2. A ella le gustaría un postre.
3. No hay bebidas en este restaurante.
4. Ella prefiere café solo.

Diálogo 3

1. María López es la presidente de Johnson Brothers.
2. María va a comer en el restaurante está noche.
3. El restaurante se llama Johnson Brothers.
4. El representante de ventas se llama James White.
5. Ellos van a comer a las 7:00 de la noche.

Actividad D: Conjugación del verbo GUSTAR

Para expresar que le gusta algo o alguien, use las siguientes formas del verbo gustar.

A mí me gusta	I like
A tí te gusta	You like (informal)
A usted le gusta	You like (formal)
A él le gusta	He likes
A ella le gusta	She likes
A nosotros/as nos gusta	We like
A ustedes les gusta	You (all of you) like
A ellos/as les gusta	They like

Note: Notice that the first part of the phrase is used for clarification purposes and may be omitted in a casual conversation.   **Ex.** *Me gusta el helado.*

Actividad E: Estudie los dibujos. Diga lo qué le gusta(n) y lo qué no le gusta.

1. El pescado	2. La carne	3. El jamón
4. Los huevos	5. El helado	6. Los camarones
7. La sal y pimienta	8. Las cebollas	9. El pollo

Actividad F: Las bebidas (Beverages) Escuche y Repita:

El agua

El té

El café

La cerveza

El jugo

El vino
(blanco,
rosado, tinto)

La leche

Actividad G: Preguntas personales: En parejas, pregunte y responda.

Ex. 1. ¿Qué te gustaría comer en el almuerzo? <u>Me gustaria comer pescado.</u>

2. ¿Qué prefieres beber en el desayuno, té, café o jugo? _____

3. ¿Prefieres una ensalada mixta o de fruta? _____

4. ¿Qué te gusta normalmente de postre? _____

5. ¿Cómo prefieres el café? ¿Solo o con crema y azúcar? _____

Estructura: Preferencias.

To state a preference, we use the verb "preferir." Look at the conjugation below and notice the spelling change. The verb **preferir** is called a stem changing e-ie verb.

Preferir	To prefer
Yo prefiero	I prefer
Tú prefieres	you prefer (informal)
Él prefiere	he prefers
Ella prefiere	She prefers
Ud. prefiere	you prefer (formal)
Nosotros preferimos*	We prefer
Ellos/Ellas prefieren	They prefer
Uds. prefieren	All of you prefer

*notice NO spelling change in the nosotros form.

Actividad H: Alimentos: Escuche y Repita:

los mariscos

el pescado

el atún

los camarones

la langosta

la carne

el bistec

el pavo

el pollo

Diga, ¿qué prefiere?

¿Los mariscos o la carne?

¿El pollo o el pavo?

¿La langosta o los camarones?

¿El pavo o el bistec?

¿El atún o el pescado?

Y su amigo(a), ¿qué prefiere?
Pregúntele.

Estructura: Another way to indicate preference is to use "*me gustaría(n)*." (I would like.)

Me gustarían los camarones, por favor.
I would like shrimp, please.

¿Te gustaría pollo o pavo?
Would you like chicken or turkey?

Actividad I: ¿Qué le gustaría comer? Diga lo que le gustaría comer en el desayuno, el almuerzo y la cena. Use las siguientes listas.

Ex: Me gustaría comer <u>jamón en el desayuno</u>.

En el desayuno	En el almuerzo	En la cena
huevos	ensalada con	carne
–fritos	–aceite y vinagre	pescado
–revueltos	hamburguesa con	arroz
jamón	–queso	papas al horno
tocino	–salsa de tomate	maíz
pan tostado	–mostaza	verduras
–con mantequilla	–mayonesa	sopa
–con mermelada	sandwich vegetariano con	pan
cereal	–queso	postre
panqueques	–lechuga	
	–tomate	
	–cebolla	
	sandwich de jamón y queso	
	papas fritas	
	Y PARA BEBER?	

En El Restaurante

Escuche y repita las siguientes palabras.

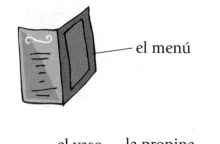
el menú

el vaso   la propina
la taza
el platillo
el tazón/pocillo
la servilleta

la cuenta

Actividad J: En el restaurante. Crucigrama

Across

1.
3.
4.
5.
7.

Down

1.
2.
3.
6.

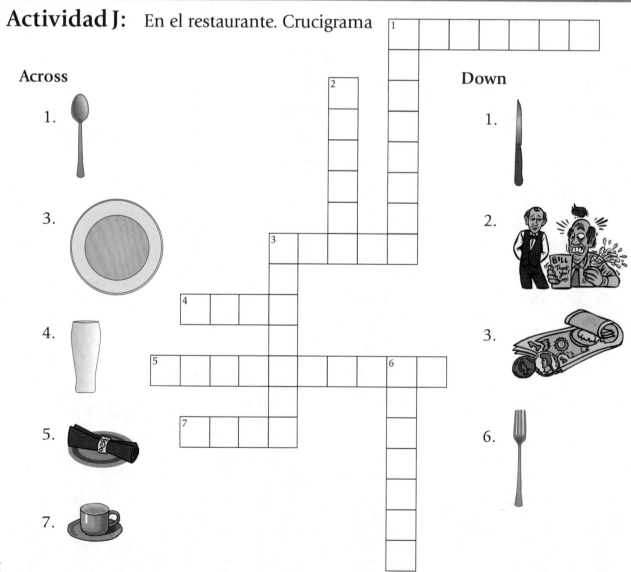

Estructura: El Futuro: IR + A + Infinitivo (going to)

To express what is going to happen, use a conjugated form of the verb to go and add the Spanish preposition "*a*" and the verb in the infinitive.

Example: Voy a comer a las dos.
I am going to eat at 2:00.

Vas a beber una soda.
You are going to drink a soda.

I am going	Voy		
You are going	Vas		comer*
He/she is going	Va		beber
You (formal) are going		+ A +	escribir etc.
We are going	Vamos		salir
They are going	Van		llamar
All of you are going			

*infinitives always end in ar, er, ir

Actividad K: ¿Qué va a hacer usted en su trabajo? Dígalo en español:

Ex. ¿Qué va a hacer Ud. mañana? <u>Yo voy a tener una reunión.</u>

¿Después del almuerzo? _____

¿El lunes? _____

¿A las 10 de la mañana? _____

¿Y su supervisor(a)?, ¿qué va a hacer él/ella? _____

Nota Cultural: Comida Española

Spanish food is chiefly Mediterranean and should not be confused with foods most Americans associate with Spanish language…tacos, burritos, enchiladas. Fresh vegetables, eggs, red meat, chicken, and fish are staples in Spain. Most fried foods are cooked in olive oil. Fresh bread is provided at every meal, usually purchased daily from the local *panaderia*.

Spain offers a variety of local specialties. Each region is known for dishes native to that area. In Galicia in northwestern Spain, one favorite is a thick soup, *caldo gallego*, consisting of meat and potatoes. In the southern region of Andalucia, you will find a classic cold soup, *gazpacho*, made from pureed cucumbers, tomatoes, olive oil, and garlic. It is served with onions, peppers, and bread.

Fish is popular, as are meat dishes, but one of the most popular choices among Spaniards is *paella*, a rice dish, yellowed by saffron and enhanced with sausage, chicken, and shellfish.

One of the most common side dishes, or *tapas*, at local bars is the *tortilla de patata*, an omelet made with eggs, diced potatoes, and onions, cooked in olive oil, sliced in wedges and served cold.

Don't look for hot sauce or tacos on Spanish restaurant menus. While people around the world share this language, they differ in many respects, including the food they eat.

 Expresiones Útiles: En el restaurante: Practique estas expresiones. Escuche y repita:

I don't have a napkin.	Me falta una servilleta.
a spoon, etc	una cuchara.
	Me faltan (plural)
The bill, please.	La cuenta, por favor.
I didn't order that.	No había pedido eso.
I would like one of those.	Me gustaría uno de esos.
Enjoy your meal.	Buen provecho.
rare	muy poco hecho. cocido(a), rojo
medium	poco hecho(a) cocido(a), término medio
well done	muy hecho(a) cocido (a), bien cocido
It's delicious.	Está riquísimo.
cheers	salud
I'm full!	¡No puedo más!, ¡Estoy lleno!

Pronunciación: Escuche y repita los ejemplos:

1. **H:** The letter H is the only letter in Spanish that is silent. It is never pronounced. Por ejemplo:

   Repita: hoy   hay   hotel   hospital   ahora

2. **LL:** The double L is usually pronounced like the English Y in the words yes or yet. Por ejemplo:

   Repita: pollo   llamo   lladró   amarillo   bello

3. **N:** The ñ is similar to the ny sound in the English word "canyon." Por ejemplo:

   Repita: compañero   mañana   año   niño   montaña

Tarea

1. Practice the dialogs at the beginning of the chapter.

2. Study the meanings and pronunciation of the vocabulary and useful expressions.

3. Make a list of 10 food items that you like the most. Say it in Spanish.

   Note: When ordering your next meal at a Mexican restaurant, use only Spanish. Practice with your server!

Vocabulario Lección 8:
Escuche y Repita.

Los Alimentos	Food
el aceite	oil
el vinagre	vinegar
la sal	salt
la pimienta	pepper
el azúcar	sugar
la mayonesa	mayonaise
la mostaza	mustard
la salsa de tomate	catsup
la mantequilla	butter
el ajo	garlic
la cebolla	onion
la lechuga	lettuce
la zanahoria	carrot
el tomate	tomato
los mariscos	shellfish, seafood
el pescado	fish
el atún	tuna
los camarones	shrimp
la langosta	lobster
la carne	meat
el bistec	steak
la hamburguesa	hamburger
el huevo	egg
el maíz	corn
la papa	potato
el queso	cheese
la sopa	soup
la verdura	vegetable, greens
el pan	bread
el pastel	pie, cake
la torta	cake
el helado	ice cream
el postre	dessert

Las Bebidas

el agua	water
el café	coffee
el jugo	juice
la leche	milk
el té	tea
la cerveza	beer
el vino	wine
blanco, rosado, tinto	white, rosé, red
la ginebra	gin
el tequila	tequila
el ron	rum
el coñac	coñac
el vodka	vodka

Drinks

En el Restaurante

la copa	goblet
la cuchara	spoon
el cuchillo	knife
el plato	plate
la taza	cup
el platillo	saucer
el tazón, el pocillo	bowl
el tenedor	fork
el vaso	glass
la servilleta	napkin
el menú	menu
la cuenta	bill
la propina	tip

In the Restaurant

Los Verbos

comer	to eat
preferir (ie)	to prefer
pedir (i)	to order/request
revisar	to check
encontrarse (ue)	to meet

Verbs

acabar de + infinitivo	just finished + infinitive
ir + A + infinitvo	going to do something
salir	to leave/go out/exit

Sustantivos

Nouns

el desayuno	breakfast
el almuerzo	lunch
la cena	dinner
el camarero	waiter
el horario	schedule
la compañía	company
los asuntos de negocios	business matters
la política de distribución	distribution policy
el/la gerente de operaciones	manager of operations
el/la agente comprador	purchasing agent
el/la representante de ventas	sales rep

Expresiones

Expressions

¿Qué hay de postre?	What's for dessert?
ahora mismo	right away!
a eso de las…	around (a certain time)
antes de	before
lo mismo(a)	same

COMMUNICATION GOALS:	To express what is happening right now To warn others of danger. To express job satisfaction.
STRUCTURE:	Acabar + de + Infinitive Estar + Present participle
PRONUNCIATION:	S C Z
CULTURAL FOCUS:	Gestures

Sabía Ud?

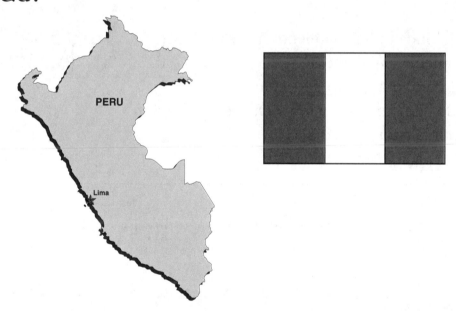

They are called *geoglyphs*, these gigantic etchings in the Earth found near Nasca, **Perú**. There are more than 1,000 of them, made perhaps by the Nasca Indians and their predecessors, the Paracas. In a region northwest of the Atacama Desert, these people created images of several animals including a whale, monkey, fox, spider, heron, hummingbird, pelican, and condor. There are human represen-tations as well, with a group of five figures suggesting a family. Scattered over more than 4,000 square miles in Peru's Pampa region, the *geoglyphs'* immense size makes them nearly indiscernable from ground level. The figures were unknown to science until airlines began flying over the region in the 1920s.

Their existence has led to debate over their origin since they were first recognized. Theories included UFO landing strips created by aliens, objects designed to appease ancient gods, astronomical calendars, or celestial observatories.

Conversación:

Escuche:

<u>Diálogo 9.1</u>

La supervisora está hablando con Linda Smith, secretaria del departamento de servicios financieros. Linda acaba de completar noventa días de prueba en la compañía.

Supervisora:	Buenos días, Srta. Smith. ¡Pase y siéntese!
Linda:	Gracias.
Supervisora:	Hoy estamos evaluando los puntos fuertes y las debilidades de su trabajo. ¿Tiene Ud. preguntas?
Linda:	El propósito es evaluar mi potencial para avanzar, ¿no?
Supervisora:	Claro. Es evidente qué Ud. tiene la habilidad y conocimiento necesarios. Aprende rápidamente. ¿Está Ud. interesada en otro puesto? La necesitamos.
Linda:	Gracias, ¡muchas gracias! Quisiera agradecerle por la oportunidad.
Supervisora:	De nada. Usted es eficiente.

<u>Diálogo 9.2</u>

El supervisor de seguridad está explicándoles a los empleados el plan de evacuación en caso de emergencia.

Supervisor:	En el nuevo manual de seguridad, hay un mapa que les muestra el plan de evacuación.
Empleado:	¿Hay una salida de emergencia en cada piso?
Supervisor:	Sí. Y también un extintor y botiquín de primeros auxilios.
Empleado:	¿Suena la alarma si hay fuego u* otro peligro?
Supervisor:	¡Claro! Y como medida de seguridad, el equipo de rescate va a recibir una llamada inmediatamente. ¡Nos preocupamos por su seguridad!

*To express the word "<u>or</u>" before a word beginning with the letter o, Spanish uses the letter **u** instead of **o**.

Actividad A: Escuche y repita: Escuche cada diálogo y repita.

Actividad B: En parejas, lea cada diálogo.

Actividad C: Preguntas para la discusión.

Diálogo 1

    1. ¿Cuándo cumple años de trabajar en la compañía?

    2. ¿Tiene Ud. una evaluación cada año?

    3. ¿Cuáles son sus puntos fuertes y sus debilidades?

    4. ¿Está Ud. interesado en avanzar a otro puesto?

Diálogo 2

    1. En su departamento, en caso de fuego, ¿cuál es el plan de evacuación?

    2. ¿Sabe Ud. dónde está el botiquín de primeros auxilios en su oficina?

    3. ¿A qué número llama Ud. en caso de emergencia?

Estructura: El tiempo presente contínuo

To tell what's happening right now, we use the present progressive tense. The present progressive consists of the present tense forms of "**estar**" + a gerund. To form the gerund, drop the ending of the infinitive verb and add the ending "**ando**" or "**iendo**"to verbs ending in "**ar**" and "**er,ir**," respectively.

Llamar	llam**ando**
Cor**rer**	cor**riendo**
Escrib**ir**	escrib**iendo**

For example, here are the present progressive forms for **llamar** (to call):

Estoy	llamando
Estás	llamando
Está	llamando
Estamos	llamando
Están	llamando

Actividad D: Use la forma correcta del verbo "**Estar**" evaluando.

1. El señor Portal _____ el potencial de los trabajadores.

2. Los supervisores _____ el talento de los empleados.

3. Yo _____ los objetivos del departamento.

4. ¿Usted _____ las responsabilidades de los gerentes?

5. La señora Smith y yo _____ el programa de seguridad.

Actividad E: En las conversaciones, busque frases en presente contínuo. Léalos en voz alta y escríbalos a continuación.

1. _____

2. _____

3. _____

Actividad F: Cambie el verbo a la forma del presente contínuo y escoja una palabra de las columnas A y C para hacer una frase completa.

Por ejemplo: ESCRIBIR = Yo estoy escribiendo el examen.

A	B	C
Yo	analizar	el examen
Tú	verificar	los cheques
Él	defender	los resultados
Ella	escribir	el informe
Usted	preparar	la cuenta
Nosotros	documentar	la evaluación
Ellos	girar	el resumen
Ustedes		

Estructura: "Just Finished" form
Acabar + de + verb in infinitive

To say that you have just finished something, we use the conjugated form of "*Acabar*" followed by the preposition "de" and then an infinitive (which tells what was just finished). The forms of *acabar* follow:

Acabo		analizar	
Acabas		verificar	(ar)
Acaba	+ de +	defender	(er)
Acabamos		escribir	(ir)
Acaban		preparar	
		documentar	

Por ejemplo: Acabo de trabajar.
I just finished working.

Paco acaba de llamar al supervisor.
Paco just called his supervisor.

¿Acabas de comer?
Did you just finish eating?

Actividad G: Llene los espacios en blanco con la forma apropiada del verbo "acabar de."

1. Yo _____ preparar los resultados.

2. Mateo _____ de verificar los nombres.

3. El botones _____ de anunciar a los invitados.

4. Los gerentes _____ de despedir a diez empleados.

5. Nosotros de _____ de celebrar el aniversario de la compañía.

Nota Cultural: Gestures

It is estimated that 60% of daily communication is unspoken. We often use gestures and body language automatically in place of or in addition to spoken language. Arms go up when we wish to hail a taxi; a teacher may silently place a finger on the lips to quiet unruly students; an exasperated mother may put her hands on her hips while waiting for a child to comply with a request. When you speak with friends, you are also aware of many subtle additions to what is actually spoken aloud. Many people speak, often animatedly, with their hands. Facial expressions may completely change the literal meaning of words, just as a change in tone or volume may provide an opposite intent.

A number of important differences exist between the United States and Spanish-speaking cultures in the way gestures and body language are perceived. In this country, most individuals find it important to maintain some distance between themselves and those with whom they speak. In Hispanic countries, people are more comfortable with less distance. Further, it would be considered rude or unfriendly to pull away from someone in Latin cultures. Latino men are familiar with brief handshakes followed by a hug; American men generally confine themselves to firm handshakes. In the United States, the "OK" symbol made by creating a circle with the thumb and index finger, is considered rude in both Spain and South America.

Argentinans consider it rude to yawn in public. You would be perceived as angry or challenging if you stood with your hands on your hips. In Chile, holding the palm upward and then spreading the fingers signals that someone is stupid, a gesture virtually guaranteeing you less-than-the-best hotel service.

Colombians avoid eating on the streets or in public places. If your waiter in a restaurant taps the underside of his elbow with the fingers of his other hand, perhaps you should consider increasing your tip … you've just been labeled stingy. If you're Paraguayan, you'd tilt your head back indicating that you forgot. Uruguayans might give the same "thumbs up" signal as Americans to indicate that everything is great. Though considered unseemly in the United States, both Mexicans and Spaniards will say "psst-psst" to catch someone's attention. Should you travel, it's nice to know that smiles are universal.

Expresiones Útiles: Practique estas expresiones. Escuche y repita:

Danger!	¡Peligro!	Help!	¡Socorro!, ¡Auxilio!
Watch out!	¡Ojo!, ¡Cuidado!	Call security!	¡Llame a los guardias!
Be careful!	¡Tenga cuidado!	Something is wrong!	¡Algo está mal!
It looks strange!	¡Se ve raro!		

Pronunciación: Escuche y repita:

1. Las letras <u>S</u> and <u>Z:</u> In Latin America the **s** and **z** are pronounced the same like the letter **s** in the English word **dress**. The English **z** sound is never used in Spanish. Por ejemplo: Repita: mesa masa zona zapato música azul

2. In Spain, the **z** is pronounced like the English **th** sound in the word **thanks**. Likewise, the letter **c** before **e** or **i** will be pronounced like the Enlish **th** sound in the word **thanks**.

3. La letra **C**: Before the letters **e** and **i**, the letter **C** is pronounced just like the English letter s in the word **Miss**. Por ejemplo:

   Repita: cinco cero cielo gracias

   In all other positions, the **c** has the English k sound like in the word **cat.** Por ejemplo:

   Repita: coca-cola como poco loco clase

Tarea:

1. Practice the dialogs at the beginning of the chapter.

2. Study the meanings and pronunciation of the vocabulary and useful expressions.

3. Look at the following expressions. Which words do you already know? Which are cognates? Which are cautionary? Which can you use to label your office? Which ones do you need to look up in a dictionary.

1.	¡No cruzar!	6.	abierto(a)
2.	¡Emergencia!	7.	¡Prohibido el paso!
3.	entrada	8.	¡No fumar!
4.	salida	9.	¡Hale!
5.	cerrado(a)	10.	¡Empuje!

Vocabulario Lección 9:
Escuche y Repita.

En la oficina	At the office
la supervisora	the supervisor
la secretaria	the secretary
el departamento	the department
los servicios financieros	financial services
los puntos fuertes	the strong points
las debilidades	the weaknesses
el propósito	the purpose
el potencial	the potential
la habilidad	the ability
el conocimiento	the knowledge
el puesto	position
la oportunidad	the opportunity
los cheques	the checks
los resultados	the results
el informe	the report
la evaluación	evaluation
el resumen	summary

seguridad	security
los empleados	employees
la evacuación	evacuation
la salida	the exit
el extintor	extinguisher
el botiquín de primeros auxilios	first aid kit
la alarma	the alarm
el fuego	fire
el peligro	danger
la medida	measure
el equipo de rescate	rescue team

Los verbos	Verbs
evaluar	to evaluate
avanzar	to advance
aprender	to learn
necesitar	to need
agradecer	to thank
respetar	to respect
explicar	to explain
mostrar(ue) muestro, muestras, etc	to show
sonar (ue) sueno, suenas, etc	to sound
recibir	to receive
preocuparse	to worry about
analizar	to analyze
verificar	to verify
defender	to defend
documentar	to document
preparar	to prepare

Expresiones	Expressions
Es evidente	It is evident.
¿Está Ud. interesado?	Are you interested?
otro puesto	another position
Quisiera agradecerle.	I would like to thank you.
Ud. es valioso(a).	You are valuable.
No podríamos lograrlo sin usted.	We can't do it without you.
el plan de evacuación	the evacuation plan
en caso de emergencia	in case of emergency
cada piso	every floor
¡Nos preocupamos por su seguridad!	We worry about your safety!

COMMUNICATION GOALS:	To make phone calls
	To take/leave messages
	To make recommendations
STRUCTURE:	Deber + infinitive
PRONUNCIATION:	Qué/Qui Gue/Gui
CULTURAL FOCUS:	Superstition and Good Luck

¿Sabía Ud?

Nicaragua is a land of lakes and volcanoes. It is the largest Central American country, slighly bigger than New York, but the most sparsely populated with only slightly more than 5 million inhabitants. Nicaragua's capital city, Managua, is located on Lago de Managua in the western portion of the country. The monetary unit is the gold cordoba, named for Spanish explorer Francisco Fernández (Hernandez) de Córdoba, founder of the first Spanish settlements in 1524, Granada and León, in what is now Nicaragua.

Conversación:
Escuche.

Diálogo 10.1

Juan Gómez está enfermo. No puede ir a su trabajo hoy. Él llama a su supervisora.

Conmutadora:	¿Aló?
Juan:	Hola, ¿Puedo hablar con mi supervisora, la señora Peña?
Conmutadora:	Lo voy a transferir a su oficina. Un momento, por favor.
	Lo siento, señor. La señora no está. ¿Puede llamar más tarde?
Juan:	No, no puedo.
Conmutadora:	¿Quisiera dejar un recado?
Juan:	Sí. Dígale qué Juan Gómez está enfermo y no puede trabajar hoy.
Conmutadora:	¿Puede repetir su nombre, por favor?
Juan:	Sí, Juan Gómez. G Ó M E Z.
Conmutadora:	Bueno, le voy a dejar su mensaje.
Juan:	Gracias, Adiós.

Diálogo 10.2

Carlos llama a la maestra de su hijo.

Secretaria:	¡Diga!
Carlos:	¿Está la señorita Hidalgo?
Secretaria:	Sí, pero no puede contestar la llamada. La línea está ocupada.
Carlos:	¿Puedo dejar un recado?
Secretaria:	Sí, ¡claro! Marque este número, 457. Espere por el tono. La señorita Hidalgo lo llamará más tarde.
Carlos:	Gracias.
Secretaria:	Adiós.

Diálogo 10.3

Juan Carlos llama al gerente de la compañía Estrella. El servicio telefónico contesta el teléfono. Pero no es la compañía Estrella; Juan Carlos tiene el número equivocado.

Empleado:	¿Aló? Compañía Gris.
Juan Carlos:	¿Puedo hablar con el señor Jones?
Empleado:	¿Con quién?
Juan Carlos:	Con el señor Jones. Robert Jones, el gerente. Estoy llamando acerca de su pedido. Es muy urgente.
Empleado:	Lo siento, señor, pero no trabaja aquí ningún señor Robert Jones.
Juan Carlos:	¿Es el número correcto: 412-3756?
Empleado:	No señor. Tiene el número equivocado.

Actividad A: Escuche y repita: Escuche cada diálogo y repita.

Actividad B: En parejas, lea cada diálogo.

Actividad C: Asociaciones: Dibuje una línea entre el dibujo y el español.

El teléfono

El número de teléfono

Contestar el teléfono

Marque este número

Un recado

Una llamada de larga distancia

El número uno ochocientos

El código de área

(800) 222-4321

(812) 555-1234
(702)

Actividad D: En parejas. Práctica Oral. Persona A = Empleado
Persona B = Supervisor(a)

Situación 1: Persona A no puede trabajar hoy. Llame a su supervisor y dígale (1) quién es. (2) qué pasa (3) que no trabaja hoy.

Persona B: (1) Saluda a persona A (2) le pregunta sobre su problema (3) le pregunta cuándo puede regresar a su trabajo.

Situación 2: Persona A no puede trabajar hoy. Persona B es el conmutador. La supervisora no está. Persona A necesita dejar un recado. Siga con la conversación.

Situación 3: Persona A no puede trabajar. Su hijo no se siente bien. Persona B es el supervisor y contesta el teléfono. Siga con la conversación.

Estructura: Should and must. Deber and debería.

To indicate what one ought or must do, use DEBER.

Yo debo	I must
Tú debes	You must (informal)
Usted debe	You must (formal)
Él debe	He must
Ella debe	She must
Nosotros/as debemos	We must
Ustedes deben	You (all of you) must
Ellos/as deben	They must

To indicate what one should do, use DEBERIA.

Yo debería	I should
Tú deberías	You should (informal)
Usted debería	You should (formal)
Él debería	He should
Ella debería	She should
Nosotros/as deberíamos	We should
Ustedes deberían	You (all of you) should
Ellos/as deberían	They should
Uds. deben	All of you should

Actividad F: Escriba la letra de la frase apropiada debajo del dibujo.

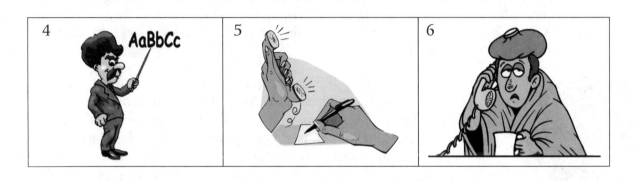

a. Debes contestar el teléfono.   d. Pablo debe comer.

b. Él debe pagar la cuenta.   e. Justo debe llamar al médico.

c. Debemos repetir el A B C.   f. Él debe dejar un recado.

Actividad G: Usando las frases de la actividad F cambie deber por debería.

a. _____   d. _____

b. _____   e. _____

c. _____   f. _____

Nota Cultural: Superstitions and Good Luck

Do you believe walking beneath a ladder will cause an accident?
Do you sprinkle salt over your shoulder to reverse misfortune or
imagine an itchy nose means you'll soon kiss a fool? These beliefs
are superstitions and are common all the world over. Superstitions
help people explain why things happen, how to cope when they do
happen, and how to avoid real and imagined unpleasantries in life.
People in Spanish-speaking countries have many superstitions, some
familiar and some unique to their circumstances.

Throughought Latin America, just as it is in North America, it is
considered bad luck when a black cat crosses your path. In Argentina, it's considered good luck when
the first of two people simultaneously saying the same thing touches the other's elbow. Nicaraguans
like to be the first to say, "*Suerta para mi!*" (Good luck for me!). A favorite Spanish saying goes, *La
suerte es ciega* (Luck is blind).

Tokens of good luck are common in Spanish-speaking countries, too. A
horseshoe with seven nail holes is considered good luck in Latin America,
just like an inverted horseshoe is in the United States. Four-leaf clovers
seem to be good luck symbols almost everywhere. Your host may not
be pleased if wine is spilled on the tablecloth, but in Latin America, it's
a token of good luck. Perhaps you've compared the serial numbers on
a dollar bill or your paycheck with friends; Hispanics find that numbers
reading the same left to right or right to left on bus tickets and lottery tickets
will bring good fortune.

Expresiones Útiles: Practique estás expresiones. Repita y Escuche:

Hurry up!	¡Date prisa!
What hard luck!	¡Qué pena!
I'm fed up!	¡Estoy harto!
I don't feel like it.	No tengo ganas.
I don't mind.	Me da lo mismo.
You're joking!	¡Bromeas!

Pronunciación: Qué/Qui – Gue/Gui

1. In the combinations qui and que, the u is silent. Qué sounds like the English letter K and qui like the English word Key.

   Escuche y repita: Quito   quince   quinientos   mantequilla

   Escuche y repita: queso   Raquel   querer   quedar   qué

2. The combination gue sounds like the English word gay. Gui sounds like ghee.

   Escuche y repita: hamburguesa   guerra   Portugues   pague

   Escuche y repita: guía   guisante   guitarra

Tarea:

1. Practice the dialogs at the beginning of the chapter.

2. Study the meanings and pronunciation of the vocabulary and useful expressions.

3. Listen to Spanish TV broadcasts and radio programs. Listen for understanding, not to translate every word.

Vocabulario Lección 10:
Escuche y Repita.

El Teléfono	**The telephone**
una llamada de larga distancia	long distance call
una llamada local	local call
el código de área	area code
el número correcto	the correct number
el número equivocado	the wrong number
el servicio telefónico	telephone service
Marque este número.	Dial this number.
¿Aló? ¡Diga! ¿Mande?	(All used to answer phone)
el tono	dial tone
el conmutador	operator
Quisiera dejar un recado.	I would like to leave a message.
la llamada	the call
la línea está ocupada	The line is busy.

Los Verbos	**Verbs**
poder (ue)	to be able to; can
yo puedo	I can
ir	to go
yo voy, tú vas etc	I go, you go, etc.
trabajar	to work
llamar	to call
contestar	to answer
transferir (ie)	to transfer
yo transfiero	I transfer (am transferring)
repetir (i)	to repeat
yo repito	I repeat

Expresiones	**Expressions**
Lo siento.	I'm sorry.
más tarde	later
dígale	tell him/her
acerca de	about
Es muy urgente.	It's very urgent.

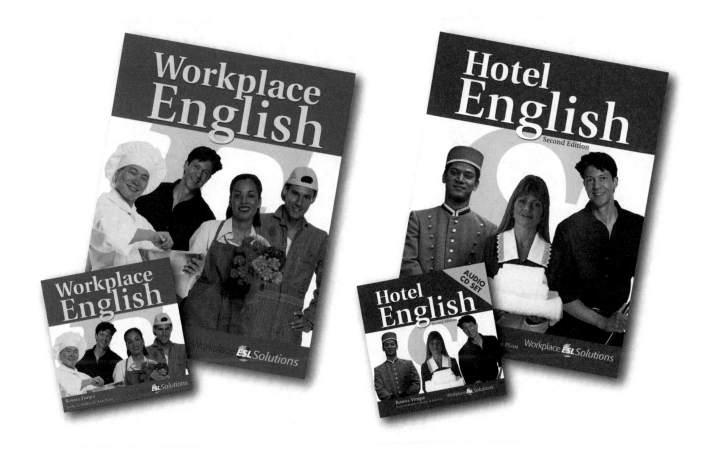

For information or to order additional
books or CDs, visit: **www.WorkplaceESL.com**
or call (702) 873-3520.